Studio Ceramics Today

Potters 6th Edition

Edited by Emmanuel Cooper
and Eileen Lewenstein

A new directory
of the work of members of the
Craftsmen Potters Association
of Great Britain.

A catalogue of the exhibition
Studio Ceramics Today
at the
Victoria and Albert Museum
Oct 6-Nov 27 1983.

Pottery Training
in the United Kingdom.

Individual entries in the CPA Directory have been written by the members concerned.
Edited by Emmanuel Cooper and Eileen Lewenstein assisted by Daphne Matthews and Marilyn Brown. Pottery training section based on information supplied by Paul Barron, David Leach, David Winkley and the colleges and potters concerned.
Cover design by Alan Humphries using detail of stoneware plate by Derek Davis.
Photographs of exhibition pots by Stephen Brayne unless otherwise credited.
The editors gratefully acknowledge help for the historical sections from Murray Fieldhouse editor of Pottery Quarterly, Robert Fournier of CPA Archives (assisted by Stella Goorney), Pan Henry of Casson Gallery and Rosemary Wren who sorted and donated early papers of the association to its archives.

Book design by Ceramic Review.

The Craftsmen Potters Association acknowledges financial help for the exhibition 'Studio Ceramics Today' from the Crafts Council.

Studio Ceramics Today
First Edition 1983
ISBN 0 9504767 3 0
Potters
First Edition 1972
Second Edition 1974
Third Edition 1975
Fourth Edition 1977
Fifth Edition 1980
Sixth Edition 1983

Published by the Craftsmen Potters Association, William Blake House, Marshall St., London W1V 1FD
©Craftsmen Potters Association 1983.
Phototypeset by Action Typesetting, Gloucester.
Printed by Billing & Sons Limited, Worcester.

Contents

Foreword

It is natural that the Victoria and Albert Museum should welcome within its walls the Craftsmen Potters Association's 25th anniversary exhibition. Set up to promote good design within the industrial arts, the Museum has had a continuing interest in contemporary crafts. It makes common cause with organisations such as the CPA which set out to promote their art by ensuring high standards. Studio ceramics is an area in which Britain has led the world, and this exhibition demonstrates the wealth of talent at work, in both traditional and innovative styles.

Roy Strong
Director, Victoria and Albert Museum

Introduction

'Studio Ceramics Today', both book and exhibition, celebrate the 25th anniversary of the incorporation of the Craftsmen Potters Association of Great Britain.

As editors of this publication and long standing council members of the association we have been closely connected with the planning and preparation of both the book and the exhibition. Our involvement with the CPA (Eileen Lewenstein was co-opted on to the council in 1957 and has been regularly re-elected; Emmanuel Cooper was elected to the council in 1969 and similarly retained) has been that mixture of delight and frustration that identifies most successful partnerships. As a co-operative, the progress and survival of the Craftsmen Potters Association, has depended upon acceptable compromise: and it is this adaptability that has proved the strength of the association.

But issues are still hotly debated and principles defended and "this sturdy band of individualists" as the *Manchester Guardian* referred to the CPA in 1958 are still capable of independent action. The council decision that 'Studio Ceramics Today' at the Victoria and Albert Museum should be a juried show prompted some members to refuse to submit work. We are sorry they are not represented in the exhibition but glad that they feel strongly enough about it to stand by their decision. Nevertheless with 105 potters showing 182 pieces this exhibition represents the wide diversity and commitment of members' interest in clay.

This book is a catalogue of the exhibition, a detailed history of the association and a record of members' work. Victor Margrie, Director of the Crafts Council and also a long standing member of the CPA, introduces the history. Rosemary Wren and Michael Casson, both of whom have been involved with the association since its early days write about its development. Stephen Brayne, who managed the shop from 1975 — 1983 describes its educational role.

The Craftsmen Potters Association was founded on a mixture of idealism, individualism and plain commonsense. These qualities are still evident today. As a co-operative, democratically elected non profit-distributing organization, the CPA has to seek out and encourage the best, but it also has to remain commercially viable. We think that the exhibition 'Studio Ceramics Today' and the continued success of the Craftsmen Potters Shop are evidence that this combination of idealism and realism is well proven and will ensure the continuing central role of the CPA in the development of studio ceramics.

Eileen Lewenstein
Emmanuel Cooper

Craftsmen Potters Association

The Craftsmen Potters Association is for me evidence of the eminent good sense of potters. What could be more sensible than a group of like-minded craftspeople coming together to share problems, to evangelise about their craft and to set up a shop to sell the product of their labours in the centre of London. It all seems so straightforward and in the spirit of William Morris that it is surprising that other crafts have not followed suit; but they have not. Of course, in reality the practical difficulties are immense, some of which are referred to by Rosemary Wren and Michael Casson, yet individual members and other devotees have appeared, almost miraculously, to overcome them. Along the way there have been disagreements which threatened the very existence of the association, but always rational counsel has prevailed and disaster avoided. In celebrating its 25 years the CPA testifies to this concerned stewardship.

The strengths of the Association are manifest but therein lies its vulnerability. A desire to maintain good fellowship has at times taken precedence over critical judgement and new developments from without the group have been regarded with suspicion and interpreted as a threat to the established order. This is not an uncommon position, though regrettable, when defining standards. I do however accept that it may be unrealistic to expect a co-operative like the CPA to seek out and give active encouragement to those potters exploring unfamiliar means of expression. Nevertheless, failure to do so has inevitably led to the Association becoming a reactive and reflective organisation rather than a radical one: equally predictably it has resulted in the alienation of a number of outstanding practitioners. Yet conversely, by adopting a policy of gradual evolution (though I doubt it was considered as such during the long hours of Council discussions) the CPA has consolidated its own position and brought countless people to a deeper appreciation of ceramics.

The educational commitment of the CPA is considerable, the lecture programme and potters' camps have been of inestimable benefit to the highly motivated amateur. Participation in these events has often been their first insight into the generosity of potters and has provided an opportunity to discuss progress and problems in an atmosphere of dynamic learning that is rarely possible in the local evening class. This willingness of professional potters to give so freely of their time to those with less experience than themselves has been central to the success of the Association in creating a dedicated audience. The importance of *Ceramic Review* should be recognized. Practical action has always dominated the thinking of the Craftsmen Potters Association and this has set it apart from other groups that had the good intentions but not the energy and will.

Victor Margrie

The First Ten Years

No one person knows of all the hard thinking, energy, enthusiasm and sheer slogging work put in by everybody else in the days when the Craftsmen Potters Association was young. To clarify my version I have chased events through the hoarded papers now before me. Here then is the start: "Minutes of the Meeting of Potters on 25th July, 1956, in connection with the Export Display at the Rural Industries Bureau".

The imposition of Purchase Tax on "household goods" was causing problems to which exporting — under licence — was the theoretical answer. Thirty-eight potters came to the meeting; none of us could previously have met so many kindred spirits at once before. Their names are listed elsewhere. Walter Lipton, RIB's Marketing Officer who had arranged it all, reported visits from 30 overseas buyers, the whole sold to a New Zealand store, a repeat asked for in South Africa. A potential market undoubtedly existed in many countries, but the Bureau could only pioneer. It was up to us to form an association that could organize a permanent display of our work and export as a group.

The minutes of the meeting that follow show a mood of developing exhilaration. A modest display of samples was soon left far behind — the most vocal potters were individualists who didn't work to sample anyway. Everyone wanted a proper Potters Centre in London but the obvious problem was finance. A Working Party of nine was appointed to deliberate, investigate and prepare a detailed Report.

Mr. F.J. Watson of Wattisfield was a third-generation flower-pot maker with 30 employees. Keith Corrigan ran the pottery at Holkham Hall with 17 employees. Reg Southcliffe's workshop made Welsh lustreware at Cregiau, Cardiff. Ray Marshall worked in partnership in Sussex. Denis Moore (Surrey) and Roger Ross Turner (Dorset) each had one helper, Helen Pincombe (Surrey) worked alone, I worked separately from my mother though together we formed The Oxshott Pottery. Our first meeting was to be on September 24th 1956, secretarial help and a meeting room being provided at first by the RIB.

Walter Lipton's assistance was invaluable. He revealed that he had helped the Furniture Makers to start a similar Association, the most suitable form being a Non Profit-sharing Industrial and Provident Society on the democratic lines laid down by Act of Parliament in 1893. We would have only to decide the Name and Objects of the Association, who should be the Members and Associates, and how the Council should be comprised. It sounded straightforward — but anyone knowing potters and the individuals concerned in particular would know that it wasn't.

The name was agreed easily. The term "craftsmen" implied a high standard of skill and background knowledge. "Craftsmen Potters", both men and women, were thereby distinguished from industrial potters. Each of us contributed something different to the "Objects". Here is Roger Ross Turner's letter eloquently pleading that each potters' technical research should be available to all, Denis Moore concerned about individual liberty and high standards (and deploring the eventual typography of the Rules), Keith Corrigan and Reg Southcliffe business-like in their suggestions for increasing sales and handling problems collectively. Mr Watson I remember as amazed at our verbosity; we respected him as the only truly traditional potter in the group. Those representing smaller workshops wanted to ensure that "work of original design and individual character" would not be overwhelmed by larger production potteries. I hoped we could make a society that everyone could feel to be a channel for sharing their own particular interests.

Views of the exhibition organised by The Rural Industries Bureau at its headquarters in Wimbledon in 1956. In the picture, bottom left, is Rosemary Wren, and in the centre Denis Moore. Walter Lipton can be seen smiling, with his arms folded in the centre of the bottom right photograph.

Defining the membership was thorny. The intention was to encourage technical freedom used with professional standards, so the first Applicaton Form stated that membership was open to all individuals or groups "possessing kilns and workshops and selling their pots to the public under an individual mark". The Rules, however give the Council absolute discretion although only a General Meeting can expel a member. With a Working Party of such diversity the "principle of non-selection" was inevitable; the "Objects" were to benefit all, not a selected few.

Denise K. Wren, my mother, was invited to the last meeting before the publicaton of the Report. Although asked to join the Working Party she had preferred to stay in the background contributing ideas and enthusiastic support; in appreciation she was made an Honorary Member on her 80th birthday in 1971. Bernard Leach was also invited to give his views; he however felt that without selection unworthy work would be promoted. He eventually accepted Honorary Membership after 1961, when the greatly increased number of pots and potters forced the reluctant decision that our Objects would be better served by a selected membership.

Finally, it was laid down that the Council members should represent workshops of various sizes and regions. We were determined not to be run by a clique.

Our report complete, an Open Meeting was held at 6, Queen's Square, Bloomsbury, London, on Saturday, February 16th 1957. The Working Party was appointed Provisional Council with the addition of a town potter, Eileen Lewenstein of Briglin.

By May 2nd a banking account was opened and subscriptions could be received: for individual potters, £3.3s.0d, for Associates £1.1s.0d, for students 7s.6d. In August the first Newsletter was sent out; there were already 50 Members and 10 Associates, Lady Leicester who owned Holkham Pottery, Norfolk, had become the first Vice-President, Reg Southcliffe and I were Vice-

POTTERY QUARTERLY

PENDLEY MANOR TRING HERTFORDSHIRE TELEPHONE TRING 2302

Display for Export. The implication that purchase tax would drive goods into the export field faced potters with the age-old problem of how a small firm can enter into foreign trade. The Rural Industries Bureau took the initiative and its Marketing Officer (O. W. Lipton) and Pottery Consultant (C. W. Bone) got together a display of 45 potteries.

This, arranged at Wimbledon, contained about 500 different items, including traditional as well as modern ordinary glazed items, stoneware and majolica, red and white clays, household articles ranging from tea or coffee sets to all kinds of cooking vessels, figurines, vases jewellery and others. Its purpose was to collect information on export markets and to book orders if possible.

Visiting overseas buyers and resident buyers for overseas firms received personal invitations, and quite a number have seen and commented on the display as well as individual items, and the various potters have been informed about this. Some sample orders have been placed and it is hoped these will result in continued business. Some more sizeable orders have also been booked, and the whole display as it stands has been sold to a New Zealand department store, which intends to exhibit it in much the same way in its own premises in the Antipodes.

At the time of writing it is intended to close the display at the end of July and make arrangements for shipment. It is thought too early to draw any definite conclusions from the experiment, but the innumerable requests to make this display permanent lead the Bureau to believe that there is a field as yet unexplored which calls urgently for a joint venture by potters themselves.

The exhibition, illustrated opposite, reported in 'Pottery Quarterly' 10, Summer 1956.

Chairmen taking the meetings alternately. Five small exhibitions were arranged — at Blakeney in Norfolk, at Holkham, at Briglin Pottery (then at 66, Baker Street, London) with a parallel display at Heal's, Tottenham Court Road, London, and at Cregiau, Cardiff.

Newsletter No.2 reports great interest at all these exhibitions. Thanks to Briglin Pottery we had made our London debut and articles had appeared in *Vogue*, the *Manchester Guardian* and *Pottery Gazette*.

On February 22nd, 1958, the Foundation Meeting of 120 people took place at the Royal Hotel, Russell Square, London. The Rules had at last been signed by us and officially registered. We must have done our work well as no need for a change has been apparent ever since. Denis Moore gave a Progress Report and, since a body of members now existed, a Council could be elected — the original Working Party/Provisional Council

FEBRUARY 1960
NUMBER 7

NEWS LETTER

**CRAFTSMEN
POTTERS
ASSOCIATION**

The cover and back of News Letter 7 showing members and friends building 3 Lowndes Court in 1959.

being asked to carry on. Michael Cardew, then Associate No. 7, working overseas, later our first Honarary Member, gave a "scintillating address".

Newsletter No.3 (April 1958) announces that the CPA now has its own Honorary Secretary, the Council having appointed Mr. David Canter. Living near Oxshott, he had been coming to my evening classes; hearing from me about CPA's urgent need for an organising secretary, he wondered if this was something he could do to help? Apparently he went to the Foundation Meeting, then on my copy of the Agenda for the following Council Meeting on March 26th, 1958, at Caxton Hall is a pencilled arrow between items 3. 'Matters Arising' and 4. 'Premises' with the scribbled insertion "David Canter". We had thought we were just trying him out on the summer exhibitions; but thus began a loyal connection, arduous and fruitful, that continued for the rest of his life.

On the way to that meeting David and I had visited Pamela, Lady Glenconner, who had offered her beautiful turquoise drawing room for a London exhibition. She immediately became a firm friend of CPA and has now been our President for many years. Her sympathy, charm and tact have been unfailing and combined with the subtly approp-

Interior view of the opening exhibition of Ray Finch stoneware.

riate wit of her literary quotations have made many an occasion sparkle.

Within a week David was sweeping those of us who lived near London along on the tide of his organizational energy. The three Summer Exhibitions were put together as one transportable Travelling Exhibition. David's first Newsletter (No. 4, July 1958) describes how he scoured Soho for potato baskets in which to transport the pots, eventually staggering up Regent Street balancing stacks of them on his head. 700 pots were entered from 45 members — of which 510 were eventually sold for a total of £307. Elegant gilt-edged cards were printed for the Glenconner show. The Council, though shocked at the price, accepted that only the best was good enough. The cost of this was balanced by frugality in other areas and the hard work of an enthusiastic band of helpers. My mother arranged the exhibits. Pamela herself "was tireless in her conducted tours" and came to know everyone's work and background. The accounts give the cost of the whole series as £183.12s.3d.

I open the file marked "Premises" — and what is this dated March 10th, 1958? Already a tentative plan for running our own shop!

Meanwhile ideas were simmering for a "Potters Day", suited to members of all sorts. It materialised at Oxshott on October 12,

Above: Outside of 3 Lowndes Court, during Ray Finch stoneware exhibition; left to right, Anita Hoy, Ray Finch, Eileen Lewenstein, Pan Henry.

The first prospectus.

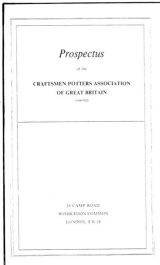

Prospectus

of the

CRAFTSMEN POTTERS ASSOCIATION

OF GREAT BRITAIN

LIMITED

35 CAMP ROAD
WIMBLEDON COMMON
LONDON, S.W.19

THE CRAFTSMEN POTTERS ASSOCIATION OF GREAT BRITAIN has been formed for the benefit of the individual potter and the small pottery workshop. The need for such a national organisation has for long been evident and can be of immeasurable benefit to all who join. It has been founded in the belief that there is a basis for mutual help inherent in craftsmanship. By greater co-operation, a wide non-selected membership and respect for individual standards, we hope to open up opportunities hitherto unexplored. There are many means by which these aims can be realised. A potential exists from which a really effective representative body can be built, and the Association should soon commence to develop the ideas outlined below:—

Headquarters

Establish a Potters Association central gallery in London for exhibitions, with a pottery shop and meeting place. Members would be entitled without a jury to select their own pottery and ceramics for sale and display (according to availability of space). Also a library and study with books on pottery and technical information, with provision for study on the spot but available also by post. Similar regional facilities are also planned.

Public Relations

Promote public relations by sponsoring articles, press correspondence, broadcasts, television demonstrations, compile a detailed directory of members and shops or retailers, circulate news and information, issue joint advertisements, establish advantageous relationships with other organisations, and promote an attitude of critical appreciation on the part of the public.

Marketing

Advise on, and assist in finding markets both at home and abroad and upon suitability of wares, advise on exporting and export formalities, customers' credit standing, hire purchase, contracts and taxation.

Official

Interpret Government orders, watch prospective legislation, keep Government departments informed on potters' views and make representations on their behalf. Advise and assist potters in any difficulty arising over conformation with laws and bye-laws. Sponsor and canvass support for any desirable changes by collective representation.

Trade Relations

Obtain concessionary terms from manufacturers for members buying equipment and materials, and/or a co-operative purchasing scheme through the Association. Arrange for insurance and legal advice.

Apprenticeship

Establish a scheme whereby employees in member potteries could qualify for documentary endorsement of their having attained a recognised standard of competence in the craft.

Overseas Liaison

Maintain contacts with fellow potters abroad, exchange news and technical information, arrange for reception of overseas visitors and introductions for members going abroad.

Membership

Full membership is open to

1. Craftsmen potters in the United Kingdom, in town and country, owning, renting or sharing kilns and workshops, and selling their pots to the public under an individual mark, sign or seal.

   The subscription for this type of full membership, that is, a craftsman potter working individually and without any full-time assistants, is Three guineas per annum.

2. Small pottery workshops in the U.K. in town and country which have no more than 30 productive employees working under one name can join as a single member. Employees producing horticultural ware are not included.

   The yearly subscription for this class of full membership is Three guineas for the pottery workshop plus an additional 10s. for each full-time worker (excluding horticultural workers) to a maximum of £6 3s. 0d.

Full membership under either of these categories will entitle each craftsman potter and small pottery workshop to participate, according to availability of space and upon a basis of equality, in all general exhibitions arranged by the Association. It entitles a full member to vote at all meetings of the Association. On joining, each full member must take up a minimum of one £1 share which is non-repayable on cessation of membership.

Associate Membership

The Association invites and will welcome as Associate members architects, scientists, teachers, painters, designers, interior decorators, sculptors, connoisseurs, collectors, curators of museums, patrons and amateurs, and all who are interested in pottery and ceramics. Craftsmen potters from abroad are especially invited.

Associate members will be entitled to such advantages as:—

1. News letter.
2. Invitations to private views.
3. Information and technical services.
4. Lectures and demonstrations.
5. Use of Centre (subject to limitations).

Subscription for Associate membership is a minimum of One guinea per annum.

Student Membership

All Students, whether at art school or under apprenticeship, are invited to join as student members at an annual subscription of 7s. 6d. for those under 21 years of age. Associate membership is available to students over this age.

It is hoped that many students and apprentices will join, as from them will come the future craftsmen potters and owners of small pottery workshops. Their views, collaboration and ideas will always be welcome, for they are in a position to be experimenting and exploring in their work ahead of the times.

Most of the advantages of Associate membership will be available to students.

Standards

The Association is founded on a non-selective basis. Knowledge of the behaviour of materials, of clays and of fire, continually increases and introduces new factors. It is believed that a spontaneous and developed art and an improved craft can be achieved and maintained only if the potter can use his techniques and create his style without constraint.

Each member's standard will therefore be the outcome of his own taste and experience in form, colour, texture, design and workmanship.

Nevertheless it is felt that beneath and beyond all differences of concept and style are seen in the work of individuals, all potters should be conscious of the essential responsibilities to their craft, and of a lively sense of fitness in tradition and design.

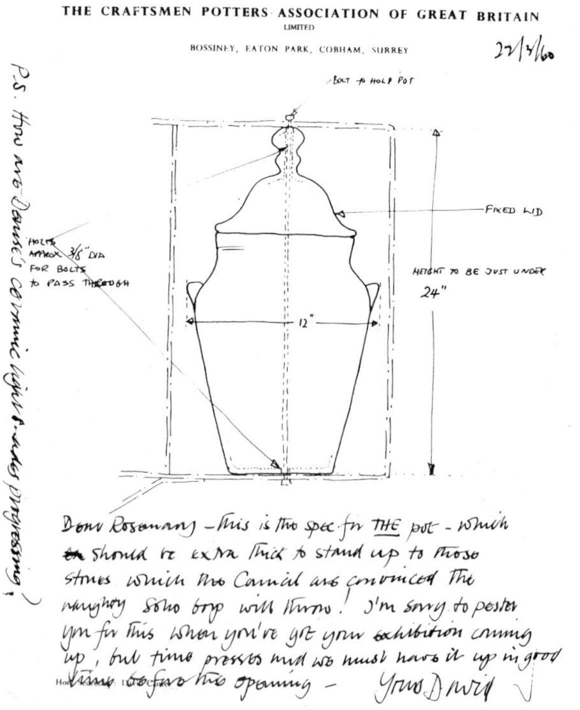

Handwritten letter in image, reading approximately:

BOLT TO HOLD POT

P.S. How are Doris's ceramic light shades progressing?

HOLES APPROX 3/8" DIA FOR BOLTS to pass through

FIXED LID

HEIGHT TO BE JUST UNDER 24"

12"

Dear Rosemary - This is the spec for THE pot - which should be extra thick to stand up to those stones which the Carnaal are convinced the naughty Soho boys will throw! I'm sorry to pester you for this when you've got your exhibition coming up, but time presses and we must have it up in good time before the opening - Yours David

A number of colourfully check-shirted figures have lately been seen deeply involved in building and carpentry operations in and around a shop in Lowndes Court, one of those inconspicuous entries on the Soho side of Regent Street. They now prove to be members of the Craftsmen Potters' Association of Great Britain, who, unpaid and unpressed, have been converting a dilapidated premises into a national showroom for their work.

Though space is restricted, the intention is that every one of the association's hundred members will get two or three cubic feet of shelf space in the basement where he can leave samples of his handiwork permanently on show. In the shop itself, a selection of members' pottery will be arranged with more regard to window-dressing techniques.

Above Top: David Canter's design for the saltglaze jar to be hung outside the Craftsmen Potters Shop, to be made by Rosemary Wren. The pot can be seen in the opposite photograph.
Above: A news report in *The Guardian*, Friday, April 22 1960 under the heading 'Potters Conversion'.
Opposite: The outside of 3 Lowndes Court.

1958 when 103 visitors examined our new saltglaze kiln, watched Mr Nixon of Wrecclesham throwing flowerpots and Mr Bateson of Ambleside throwing big pots; there was a visit to a collection of Persian pots — and at "Pinewoods" nearby "Talking, mixing and generally getting to know more potters than you would normally see in a year". Finally there was 'cello music from Denis Moore accompanied by David's wife Kay (who must have been exhausted after organising all those meals) and folk songs from Chris Charman of Godshill Pottery. Sheila and Mick Casson were there and his report ends "May the CPA have many more such days ahead!" which indeed we had. They were almost all organised by David Canter.

Later came the monthly Evening Meetings. The list speaks for itself of the generosity of time and thought put into them by so many speakers. Some took the form of an Annual Party at a London exhibition or museum. From 1960 — 1964 they were my responsibility, then Murray Fieldhouse took over.

Mick's sister Pan Henry was at that first Potters Day too. We were amazed and delighted to hear that she was prepared to manage our hypothetical shop. Also my mother brought forth an idea with a different emphasis for financing a shop: each potter contributing £5 to a Premises Fund would be entitled to take over a specially designed exhibition corner for a week. Their personal invitations would build up publicity, their demonstrations could add unique interest, they would learn about the shop. Everyone was in favour, eventually 48 people booked exhibitions and a total of 74 people contributed.

CPA's first official AGM was on April 4th, 1959. As Chairman of the Council I could announce that premises had been found!

The first Craftsmen Potters Shop was at 3, Lowndes Court, Carnaby Street, in central London. About 20 people worked on its transformation during the year following for a

Pan Henry and David Canter in the Craftsmen Potters Shop,
3 Lowndes Court.

total of 950 hours and more, but the brunt of the work was done by Mick Casson, Pan Henry (who did all the painting), Lawrence Keen, Anita Hoy, Eileen Lewenstein, Aubrey Coote and of course David Canter who designed and co-ordinated. Eventually with elegant window and general display, carefully thought-out solus exhibition space and office on the ground floor, member's room and compartments for work of their own choice downstairs — there it all was just as we had dreamed.

On May 28th, 1960, two hundred people crowded in. Walter Lipton, justly proud, introduced Lady Glenconner who made a brilliant opening speech surrounded by a distinguished 'Special Exhibition' from Ray Finch. A financial success from the day of opening, with an astonishing average of £80 a week retail sales reported by December, it remained our home with Pan as manager for seven years.

By 1967 all available space was overflowing with pots and association office work: sales averaged £327 a week. We had to admit that our first shop was outgrown and look towards the possibility of even greater development in new and larger premises more prominently situated.

Rosemary D. Wren

The CPA 1967-1983

Taking a broad view it is possible to see, as Rosemary Wren explains in the preceding article, that the first ten years of the Craftsmen Potters Association was a time of great achievement. Through the enthusiasm of its members led by David Canter as Honorary Secretary, and backed by the organisational and selling skills of Pan Henry, the shop manager, the ideal of a co-operative for potters run as far as possible by potters was brought into existence. Since moving into the present shop in Marshall Street sixteen years ago a rather different picture emerges. For the CPA the last few years of the 60s was a time of consolidation on which a sound reputation was built. But the next phase, say from the mid-70s onwards, showed the Association reflecting more and more the changes taking place in ceramics throughout the world and emerging in the 80s as the representative organisation for a wide spectrum of potters.

In December 1967 the CPA moved to its present premises in William Blake House on the corner of Broadwick and Marshall Streets, just a stone's throw from Carnaby Street. David Attenborough opened the new shop to a packed house of enthusiastic potters and public. The negotiations with Westminster Council carried out by the indefatigable David Canter were long and complicated and at their conclusion the hoped-for gallery area that was to have complemented the shop had to be abandoned because of the expense entailed. As with the first shop David designed the interior layout in a style appropriate to the times, English oak and warm clay tiles predominating. It is only right that today, a decade and a half later, the new design of the shop by Ron Carter, recently completed with the help of a grant from the Crafts Council, should reflect the needs of the 80s. If the building of the first shop was largely in the hands of three people, David Canter, Lawrence Keen and

myself, ably helped by volunteers, it is true to say that this spirit still prevailed in 1967. Many potter members, and in particular Harrow students, helped David Canter (still of course in the thick of it all) even though professional builders were called upon for much of the work. It should be recorded that those who worked in the shop found it a delight; it showed off the pots, particularly the stonewares of the late 60s and early 70s to great advantage.

These last sixteen years have seen many changes in the potters' world and merely to list the CPA events and exhibitions conveys only a flavour of the times. Robert Fournier, CPA archivist has been an excellent source of reference. Attempting to record impressions of the Association through these years means I can only mention a few of the people and happenings which produced, in all, a remarkable period of growth and expansion.

Over the whole of the 25 years there have been nine council members elected by their peers to become chairperson at meetings held four times a year. Their duties did not end with Council meetings but were concerned with detailed policies as well as more general planning; all of them except Jane Hamlyn the present Chairwoman worked closely with the honorary secretary and treasurer David Canter. Looking at this list of names, and recalling just a few of the other council members, it is evident that throughout its existence the Council has represented a healthy cross section of potters working with clay in very different ways. But to return to the "chair", after Rosemary Wren there was myself, David Leach, Colin Pearson, Eileen Lewenstein, David Eeles, David Lloyd Jones, George Rainer and now Jane Hamlyn. Council members not only reflected as far as possible geographical representation (great efforts were made earlier to fulfil this ideal) but the various areas of ceramics: hand-building, throwing, repetition, education

Pan Henry in the newly opened Marshall Street shop.

and moreover, robust to meticulous, functional to sculptural uses of clay.

A 1967 Council list had 'Beano' Katharine Pleydell-Bouverie, Brigitta Appleby, Harry Horlock Stringer, Colin Pearson, Murray Fieldhouse, Alan Wallwork, Eileen Lewenstein, David Leach, Anita Hoy, Bryan Newman, John Reeve and Rosemary Wren with myself as Chairman — a pretty varied 'bunch' to work with. Six or seven years later people like Peter Dick, Colin Kellam, Mary Rogers and David Winkley were there. It was David Winkley who recently took over as Treasurer and used his expertise at a time of considerable crisis after David Canter's tragic death. The CPA was indeed lucky to have such a cool head to call upon from its ranks of potters. During the later 70s and into the 80s the diversity and variety can be seen by looking at the lists of potters who put their ideas and energies at the service of the CPA in response to the membership who voted them onto the Council. You could see the organisation grow and broaden under their influence.

There have been three managers or directors of the shop during this time. Pan Henry continued in Marshall Street until 1972 when Chris Palmer took over for three years until Stephen Brayne came in 1975. Each has been concerned with the day to day running of the shop and the affairs of the Association; they have all been lucky to have had dedicated staff. Pan Henry had the additional task before the days of *Ceramic Review* of getting together a regular Newsletter. In theory this was prepared by various Council members but more often than not it was a last-minute compilation job of contributions by various members and friends which was put together by Pan and her loyal staff. When Emmanuel Cooper and

Eileen Lewenstein said in 1969 that they thought the time had come for a more professional magazine which they offered to edit, it gave the Association a new and important publishing function. The first issue appeared in January 1970. *Ceramic Review* confirmed the outward looking qualities of the Association and responded to the ever widening interest in studio pottery.

Potters also began to respond to changes in the market, adapting to different tastes and styles. The late 60s was the heyday of the repetition domestic pot, often handsomely glazed with creamy white dolomite and black iron tenmoku. Customers regularly bought sets of pots, purchased goblets by the hundreds and mugs by the thousands. Ceramic sculpture, for even then no one really knew what to call it, was on display and found a small but devoted market with Gordon Baldwin, Bryan Newman and Alan

Wallwork continually coming up with new ideas and forms. By the early 70s potters who had trained at pottery courses such as those at Harrow School of Art were able to earn a living from making domestic pots. Often they relied on sales from the CPA shop for a considerable part of their incomes.

But by this time the shop had gained a reputation which brought managers and directors of shops and galleries from all over the world to make selections of work; export orders were negotiated as far afield as Australia, USA and Japan. All of this continues today, but ten years ago gradually, and then with gathering momentum it marked further changes in the Association. The range of work has widened, colours have changed and new styles have appeared. Side by side with repetition domestic stoneware, toasted unglazed surfaces or celadon glazes, there are more decorative earthenwares and

Above: Inside of the Marshall Street shop, which was designed by David Canter to make full use of natural surfaces. The window arch reflects the shape of the kiln arch.
Opposite: The display stands in the shop.

colourful stonewares plus many one-off pieces, vessels as well as sculptural forms; above all perhaps it is the advent of porcelain that has given a different look to the shelves and general display at the CPA in the 80s, and for that we have to thank David Leach more than anyone else; his throwable medium temperature procelain body has been available commercially since the early 70s.

Activities taken on by the CPA have helped to put pots and potters before a wider public. Communication has been the keynote, achieved through exhibitions, evening meetings and many other sorts of 'events'. Potters, full-time and part-time, professional, experienced, students and amateurs have contributed to and become aware and informed of the latest ceramic ideas. Over the last sixteen years for instance exhibitions have ranged from the major 'solus' shows taking up the whole of the display space of the shop, to group exhibitions, window displays and 'theme' shows like cooking pots, teapots, candlesticks or boxes. Exhibitions have been arranged to coincide with the publication of new books by full members; and have included Alan Caiger-Smith's book 'Tin Glaze Pottery in Europe and the Islamic World' in 1973.

Most recently Peter Lane's book 'Studio Ceramics' was launched in an exhibition of work by over 50 potters. Groups of potters outside the CPA have been invited to exhibit: the South Wales Potters, itself brought into existence by help from the CPA and its South Wales member Frank Hamer; or groups of potters from Canada, France and Germany. In recent years the 'New Members' show has become a regular feature demonstrating the growth of the Association and its seeking out and acceptance of new ideas. The CPA took on the daunting task of helping to arrange the International Exhibition of Ceramics at the Victoria and Albert Museum in 1972. My memory has not faded yet of one of the judges, Hans Coper, leaning back, perhaps swooning might be a better word, at the sight of hundreds and hundreds of pots and 'objects' unpacked and sitting on top of their wrappings waiting for us to 'judge' them.

Evening meetings, wide ranging in subject matter and usually by experts, have often been held, appropriately, at the Art Workers Guild. Recalling just a few gives the flavour of these events, which have helped to give information, spread understanding about pottery and generally delight a growing number of people — not only potters by any means. In 1967 Michael Cardew gave three talks on 'Pottery in West Africa' while Daniel Rhodes spoke about the *avant garde* pots of the United States. Two years later Emmanuel Cooper, Robert Fournier and Derek Royle headed a 'brains trust' on technical matters, to be followed later that year with one on

Above Top: Outside of present shop in Marshall Street (Broadwick Street window) designed in 1983 by Ron Carter.
Above: View of members' stock shelves which retain the principle that, once elected, members can send work of their own choice.
Opposite: The centre stands in the present shop.

Workshop Practice with Harry Horlock Stringer, David Eeles, Barbara Cass and Peter Dick. In 1974 Bob Rogers stimulated much thought when he spoke about 'Freedom and Design in Craft', whilst in 1967 Tony Hepburn showed Modern American Ceramics, followed in 1977 with Bill Ismay on "A Collector's Point of View". And so forth on every conceivable aspect of how to use clay, glaze, fire — and why.

Other events too, have helped to bring potters closer together whilst letting a wider and wider circle of people know about pottery. When Bernard Leach finally agreed to join the CPA as an Honorary member he said he was joining us because we had 'good fellowship' — an important part of the make-up of the Association. Events such as the 1968 'Potters Day' hosted by Harry Horlock Stringer at Taggs Yard have been significant in their way. 'Potters Days' led on to David Canter's idea of the 'Potters Camps': three were held at Loseley Park, Surrey, two at Dartington, Devon, (including the mammoth multi-craft — wood, glass, calligraphy, textiles) — from 1973 to 1982. These occasions have proved immeasurably popular and have helped foster the caring CPA image. Meetings for full members and associates at Dillington House, Somerset, Dartington, Devon and above all at West Dean, West Sussex have proved that potters can relate to each other across a spectrum that ranges now from functional domestic and garden ware to innovative one-off ceramics. Long may this communication continue. Film festivals, demonstrations of potting techniques in the shop, and more, extend the list of activities showing a similar commitment.

The Silver Jubilee Exhibition at the Victoria and Albert Museum makes the point again that all the efforts over the years have helped to establish new standards of excellence, both technical and aesthetic. This aim has always been a major concern of the CPA and one story illustrates the at times

Michael Casson finishing one of his jugs on the wheel.

anguished struggles members have faced in improving the quality of work (sometimes selection processes literally took all day and all night). I have a memory of a meeting the Council called to try and find a definitive way of judging work. We invited Denise Wren and Bernard Leach, the doyens of their day, to come along to our meeting and tell us how they thought work should be judged. Denise Wren in an amazing piece of critical analysis had listed several categories under which a pot could be judged and each category had many questions or points that could be asked about the work. I remember a figure of 87 points; it was a brilliant piece of planning. Bernard Leach thought a judge should ask one question 'has the pot - heart'! The meeting ended, eventually, and the CPA has tried ever since to enquire what is a good pot? what is a good piece of work?

While all this heart searching and questioning was proceeding inside the CPA the world of ceramics outside was changing. The CPA did not ignore these developments. Membership over the years has reflected differences in education, in market demands and reactions to outside influences such as the first sightings of ceramics from the USA in 1960.

In the world of education which I believe to be a major influence in shaping ceramics there have been crucial changes. Sixteen years ago Dip.A.D. was giving way to more scholarly based BA (Hons) courses. Vocational training courses such as the one which sprang up at Harrow School of Art, as well as in other schools responded to a need. In the event, innovative ceramics and domestic pottery were both well served. Hans Coper was teaching at the Royal College of Art and a small but significant group of potters was about to emerge from there in the early 70s. Since then the number of BA (Hons) centres continued to grow and the cumulative effect of this and a number of other new factors has had far-reaching results today in the 80s.

In 1971 Lord Eccles set up the Crafts Advisory Committee, later to be the Crafts Council, which was headed by potter Victor Margrie. The 'brief' was to promote the artist-craftsman and stimulate growing public awareness of crafts. The Crafts Council has always helped both traditional and innovative craftspeople especially the young — this is their investment in the future of crafts. By the mid 70s 'Crafts' magazine alongside 'Ceramic Review' and a growing body of literature about ceramics was showing an increasing number of 'new ceramics' as well as traditional forms. Galleries selling 'individual' pieces rather than repetition domestic ware were starting up all over the country. At the Victoria and Albert Museum the Crafts Council opened a Craft Shop and other centres followed. Sotheby's started to take an interest in crafts as Fine Art. The market had changed.

Late in the 70s the economic recession seemed to underline these new forces at work in our pottery community. All these factors though lying beyond the control of the CPA or indeed anyone have nevertheless been reflected in the Association itself; by the influx of new kinds of potters to its ranks, the changing display facilities and, this year in a completely new refurbishment. It would need a Maynard Keynes of the ceramic world to evaluate how the confluence of these events, education, promotional, economic and aesthetic have affected and influenced each other. Which came first the buyer or the pot? Through all these changes, the CPA has not only survived but grown in stature. It has to thank the hard work of its members, the support given by a host of associate members and friends and the guidance received from people like David Canter. With a fine new shop showing a splendidly wide range of work (and a new manager) long may it flourish, and long may potters of all kinds meet and hold dialogue with each other.

Michael Casson

The Educational CPA

If the CPA had done nothing else over the last quarter century but successfully establish a centre in the West End of London for exhibiting and selling the work of its members, then it would have played an important role in the development of contemporary ceramics. There is little doubt that The Craftsmen Potters Shop offers the visitor from this country, or abroad, the opportunity for seeing a broad cross-section of ceramic work currently being made in this country. The CPA, however has never contented itself with this role. From the earliest days it has been engaged in spreading information about techniques of pottery making through lectures, seminars, demonstrations and workshops. Many aspects of ceramics have been covered, from clay preparation, throwing, slabbing and handbuilding to decorating, glazing, kiln building and firing. This extraordinary sharing of technical information from the very highest professional sources has been almost unparalleled in other crafts and is certainly a major contribution to the ever increasing

Potters Camp 1973

understanding and appreciation of contemporary ceramics.

One of the earliest Newsletters notes that even before the first Craftsmen Potters Shop opened at Lowndes Court, there had already been 'Potters Days'. In October 1959 at Pinewoods, Oxshott, the programme included a lecture by Peter Stoodley describing his coke and drip-feed oil kiln, a lecture on saltglaze by William Gordon, who had advised on the firing of the salt kiln at the Oxshott Pottery, a talk on European slipware and a symposium on glazes headed by Paul Barron and Henry Hammond. As well as the lectures there were also demonstrations of throwing by Roger Ross Turner and Rosemary Wren, copious food and drink and, of course the invaluable, informal exchange of information that inevitably takes place when potters meet and eat. The event was attended by both Full and Associate members of the Association so setting the pattern for many successful events that followed.

Potters Days proliferated and grew in scope

Top Left: Jane Hamlyn, now Chairwoman of the CPA, demonstrating paper resist methods.
Top Right: Harry Davis decorating a pot on the wheel.
Above Left: Walter Keeler firing raku in the kiln built at Potters Camp.
Above Right: David Winkley brush decorating a pot watched by Sheila Casson and David Canter.

and format over the years, and were attended by ever growing numbers of members, paralleling the steady growth of the Association itself. Today a regular pattern has emerged. Weekend demonstrations and workshop events are organised in such sympathetic surroundings as West Dean College, Dillington House, Dartington Hall and Loseley Park. 'Potters Camp' started in 1973 at Loseley Park where some 340 members braved the rigours of canvas to watch many of the country's leading potters at work. All activities were housed in huge marquees and banked seating was arranged around an arena where the potters worked to give the audience a better view. Michael

Casson acted as Master of Ceremonies — a role he was to perfect over the years — taking questions from the audience and turning them into debates.

So successful was this idea that it became the blueprint for CPA camps, and also for similar events organised by the Northern Potters and the North and South Wales Potters. Behind the success of the CPA Camp was the undoubted organisational genius of David Canter. He seemed able to marshall marquees, catering, demonstrators and supply of materials and equipment with such ease that it belied the enormous amount of planning and sheer hard work required. The Dartington Craft Camps of 1977 and 1979 developed from Potters Camp and were multi-craft versions of the same model; visitors were able to see not only potters but also weavers, wood-turners, calligraphers, jewellers, batik-makers, glass blowers and blacksmiths demonstrating their skills.

In 1982 Potters Camp returned to Loseley Park, reverting to a single craft event. The concept of participatory workshops for members, which had been introduced at Dartington in 1979 for the first time, was fully implemented, and a programme of four workshops a day was organised in which groups of up to a dozen were able to work with full members. Such workshops now form the basis of every weekend event and all materials and equipment are provided, giving associate members, many of whom are student and amateur potters, a chance to confer with leading professional potters, and benefit from their experience.

Another aspect of the CPA's educational activities has been the regular series of Evening Meetings that has been organised since the earliest days of the Association. The very first of these followed soon after the opening of the Lowndes Court shop, with Michael Casson giving a talk and demonstration on 'Handles, spouts, lips and knobs' to an audience of thirty five members.

It is interesting to speculate on the numbers that such a talk would attract today.

Rosemary Wren explains some of the original principles behind these meetings in the same Newsletter when she suggests that "exchanging experience will increase our awareness and should help us all to make better pots." The realisation was already there that calling in outside "experts" to deliver lectures was superfluous — CPA members themselves had a far greater body of knowledge than any one expert could ever have. Indeed, the second and third Evening Meetings served to underline this point; the first, a lecture by Michael Cardew on Nigerian potters, and the second, Bernard Leach talking about "the Three Friends, as the Chinese call brush, ink and paper, and about pattern making and its marriage to form." The many distinguished speakers that have followed are listed on page 203. No aspect of ceramic art has been overlooked from the practical and the aesthetic to the historical and the philosophical.

The programme continues today. The latest in a long line of residential weekends at West Dean was held in September 1983 and Evening Meetings are arranged well into 1984. A series of Workshop Open Days are planned when full members welcome associate members to tour their workshops for a day, providing demonstrations and opening the way for informal discussions. Plans will soon be under way for the next Potters Camp. 'Studio Ceramics Today' the 25th Anniversary Exhibition of the Craftsmen Potters Association at the Victoria and Albert Museum, is accompanied by a programme of lectures and demonstrations, perpetuating the aims of the pottery pioneers who established the Association in the late fifties, not merely to sell pottery, but to promote general appreciation and awareness of the craft.

Stephen Brayne

Two Members Comment

Two members comment on their Membership of the Craftsmen Potters Association. Katharine Pleydell-Bouverie, one of the founder members, continues to pot in her 80s: Andrew McGarva is at the start of his career as a potter.

To those of us who work from choice in remote parts of the country and probably turn a rather dubious eye on London, the CPA shop is likely to be one of the pleasanter parts of it. One sees one's fellows' pots there; one sometimes sees one's fellows; and one invariably meets with friendly advice and information on whatever one wants from everyone in charge. It is the same with the Association in general and its admirable journal *Ceramic Review*. Indeed, looking back a long time I find it difficult to remember, or even imagine, what we did without them. So — cheers for David and Pan, who carried the burden of so much of the first years, for them who do it now, and for the CPA as a whole.

Katharine Pleydell-Bouverie

In Britain, not many people seem to want handmade objects of high quality. Pottery and other craft traditions have faded through changing circumstances. Society moves on, and thankfully leaves behind the awful working conditions of most traditional craftworkers. So, if today's homes seem to lack quality it is for craftspeople to try and influence their owners. Through the work they do and by forming or joining groups they can let people know what alternatives are available. We, in the rich countries of the world, are about to see great changes in our way of life. I think we still need objects which are part of a cultural continuity, made for us now, but made taking note of what has gone before. A pot, whether we like it or not, is a statement of attitudes and a reflection of culture. It is so commonplace it might be thought irrelevant; it is not, because it is so commonplace.

By nature I am not a joiner of clubs, so why did I join the CPA? One reason was to reach the widest possible public through selling my work in the Marshall Street shop. When embarking on a career of making things few people want or value, we can all benefit by being part of a larger group. The CPA is democratic; if I do not agree with its policies, it is for me to use my vote accordingly. It is criticised for being elitist — nothing is perfect — but it has raised standards over the years, by having a policy of selection.

'Craftsmen Potters'? — of course, there are none of these left, and now we must all be more or less artists working with clay. Compared to traditional potters, the present level of skill in Britain is low, due largely to the lack of demand for handmade pots. So is pottery an anachronism? I believe not, despite the current anti-pot anti-skill fashion. There is a limit to the number of flat teacups one wants on one's mantlepiece. The history of ceramics has taught us that what clay can be used for *par excellence* is making vessels. As a sculptural medium, it is very expressive on a domestic scale, but has always proved lightweight, and down-market. Contrary trends are temporary.

The CPA was set up by potters for potters, and so it remains, though over the years its role has altered. I have visited countries where there has been no such organisation, we are certainly better off with it than without it. Now it is so large, it seems sometimes to move rather slowly, but I think that it is probably a good thing — it avoids the slavish following of fashion, and gives a broad and, I hope, a balanced approach. I am glad the best shop in the country for buying pots still belongs to potters.

Pottery is similar to gardening or music. Pots, like plants, come up the same each year; if they are healthy they will always be fresh. Occasionally new varieties are introduced; if there is an imbalance in the soil one kind of plant will dominate. But then, that is what makes it continually interesting. Musicians know that however often the same piece is played, it is never the same. They also know that to learn to improvise one must have a great depth of knowledge and skill. Me — I just keep practising, and I hope others will continue to do the same. The CPA can help us do it.

Andrew McGarva

Studio Ceramics Today

All full members of the Craftsmen Potters Association were invited to submit three recent pieces for the exhibition. From the 300 or so pieces submitted the selection committee consisting of Victor Margrie (Director Crafts Council), Oliver Watson (Department of Ceramics, Victoria and Albert Museum), Emmanuel Cooper (Potter and Writer) and David Frith (Potter) chose 182 pieces by 105 potters. As an introduction to the exhibition Oliver Watson writes about the collection of studio pots in the Victoria and Albert Museum.

The Victoria and Albert Museum and Studio Ceramics

To attempt to describe the Museum's collection of studio pots begs the prime question: what is a studio pot? It is a question that is easy to answer now: studio pots are the work of those potters who identify themselves as 'studio potters', through adherence to groups such as the Craftsmen Potters Association, or by other means. Defining the Museum's collections which grew up in correspondence with the growth of what is now recognizable as a movement, presents greater problems. Studio potting — in its widest meaning of small-scale non-industrial work — has a long history in this country, stretching back far beyond the return of Leach from Japan in 1920, and possibly going back further still in France, to the first half of the nineteenth century. In our galleries the English earthenwares and stonewares are displayed in chronological order from the Medieval period. Our collection of studio ceramics forms a natural continuation of the displays of late Victorian 'Art' pottery (the Martin brothers, Sir Edmund Elton etc); of country wares (Brannam and the Fishleys) and more urban, self-consciously 'studio' work (Reginald Wells, the Omega workshops, Gwendoline Parnell and the Chelsea ladies). Here the work of Leach, Cardew, Staite Murray and their successors can be seen in its true context as a tremendous revitalisation of older concepts, concerns, and traditions.

In ordering the collection we are forced to make arbitrary boundaries that may make no sense historically or aesthetically. I include here, for example, Charles Vyse's vessels but not his figures, and include the Omega products but not Brannam's or Fishley's. After about 1930, the position becomes clearer, with the growth of a more clearly identifiable group of potters, with something, though often bitterly disputed, of a group philosophy.

The collection is small in comparison to the Department's total of over 60,000 pieces, numbering some 750 pots, representing over 150 British and about 55 continental potters. The collection naturally has substantial numbers of pieces by potters now regarded as the great masters (and mistresses) of the craft: 38 pieces by Bernard Leach (and a further 33 by his pottery and family), about 30 pieces by Michael Cardew (including a good number of his pre-war earthenware from Winchcombe), 25 pieces by William Staite Murray, 35 pieces by Lucie Rie, though, to our regret, only a dozen by Hans Coper. The collection has interesting collections of early pioneering figures — Reginald Wells, Denise Wren and others whose names are not so well-known, such as Frances Richards. There is a group of pieces by people who are primarily artists in other media — Picasso, Piper, Duncan Grant and Vanessa Bell. From the 1950s onwards we are able to represent a broad cross-section of work by a large number of potters, some of whom are still known, others of whom were evidently of more transient interest. The collection as a whole contains a good number of great masterpieces, and a pleasingly high proportion of top quality work. It also contains pieces that are frankly bad, or only of interest as examples of "period style". This is how a national and historical collection should be.

Over one third of the pieces are on display, in cases which, for want of space, are often sadly overcrowded. The collection was formed largely by the now defunct Circulation Department which fell victim to the Government's public spending cuts in 1977. This Department organized travelling exhibitions which toured the country, and pieces were purchased with particular shows in mind. The idea of forming a balanced collection through which general development and divergent streams could be illustrated was not however lost. It is much to the credit of Hugh Wakefield and David Coachworth after him that the collection is as representative and as excellent as it is.

Circulation Department's responsibilities were taken over by the Ceramic Department which now adds to the collection at the rate of some 40-50 pieces a year. Pieces are acquired in a number of ways, through bequests and gifts, but mostly through purchase, either direct from the artists or at galleries. A good proportion of the yearly acquisition is not contemporary work, but historic, as we find opportunities to fill gaps in our past collecting. We have thus recently received a most generous gift from Lucie Rie, who after her greatly successful retrospective exhibition in 1982, gave us the best of her pre-war work from Vienna. We also purchased a group of her recent pots, to complete what must be one of the most excellent and most representative collections of her work. Similarly in recent years we have purchased a group of pieces by Denise Wren, a potter who was hitherto but scantily represented in the collections, and a group of pieces done at the Bullers factory by Anita Hoy. Gaps in our holdings become more apparent as time passes, and we are concerned to see these filled.

Purchasing absolutely contemporary work is the most contentious of all. Sooner than buy indiscriminatley across the board in the hope of covering all the major figures, or figures that will later turn out to be major, we rely on the sole criterion of conviction — conviction of the member of staff (not always the same individual) proposing the acquisition that the piece adds to the collection in a positive fashion. Sooner a piece hated by many but loved by one, than a piece chosen as a compromise by a committee. There is a rough "shopping list" of potters desired, but we prefer to wait, rather than represent by second-rate pieces.

There are now limitations on our collecting of a sort not encountered before — only a few years ago a price of over £100 was a rarity; we now often pay £500 and more for leading artists. Much of the work now tends to the sculptural, and some of extremely large size. Even smaller sculptural pieces need more space in a showcase than an equivalent sized teapot. Our policy so far has been to show as much as possible at the expense of optimum display for individual pieces — a policy whose disadvantages and advantages are often brought home to us by complaints from the public. The sculptural tendencies bring further problems — those of demarcation. Is it the function of the V & A, primarily a Museum of decorative art, to collect modern sculpture? Should this be left to other institutions and, if so, which? Another issue, little discussed so far but of increasing importance, is that of relating the V & A's national collecting policy to those of other institutions. The Crafts Council, the Crafts Study Centre at Bath, and a number of provincial museums are very active collectors, and in the near future closer communication would be in the interests of all.

The fundamental aim of the Museum's collection of studio pottery, is not only to be able to show the best examples of current work by the leading potters; but to do so in a setting that clearly shows its historical context. Gallery 138, in which the 25th anniversary show itself is held, will, it is hoped, allow us greater scope for better display. Soon we shall be able to stage temporary exhibitions of our more recent acquisitions whose contents change with our continuing purchases. This will, we hope, allow us to pay better regard to the fastest growing and in many ways the most exciting part of our Department's collections.

Oliver Watson
Department of Ceramics

Pots illustrated in this catalogue section are indentified in the captions with an *.

Chris Aston
1. Porcelain bottle, sang de boeuf. 11 cm.
2. Stoneware bottle, sang de boeuf. 17 cm.
3. Stoneware bottle, sang de boeuf. 22 cm.*

Ruth & Alan Barrett-Danes
4.   Predator pot, porcelain, thrown and modelled.
5.   Predator pot, porcelain, thrown and modelled.

Paul Barron
6.   Flower vase, thrown and modified form. Black and white poured glazes.

Val Barry

7. Tall sentry, beige and black, stoneware.*
8. Tall sentry, black and white, semi-porcelain.*
9. Tall figure, black and white, semi-porcelain.

Michael Bayley
10.   Large bowl, agate and inlaid stoneware.

Peter Beard
11. Stoneware bowl with manganese decoration over white slip. 1260°C.

Terry Bell-Hughes
12. Mixing bowl with added lip, stoneware.*
13. Ash glaze teapot, stoneware.

Maggie Berkowitz
14. Cat on the Mat. Stove back and floor ironstone tiles, painted decoration.

Audrey Blackman
15. "A seat in the Sun" porcelain bisque.

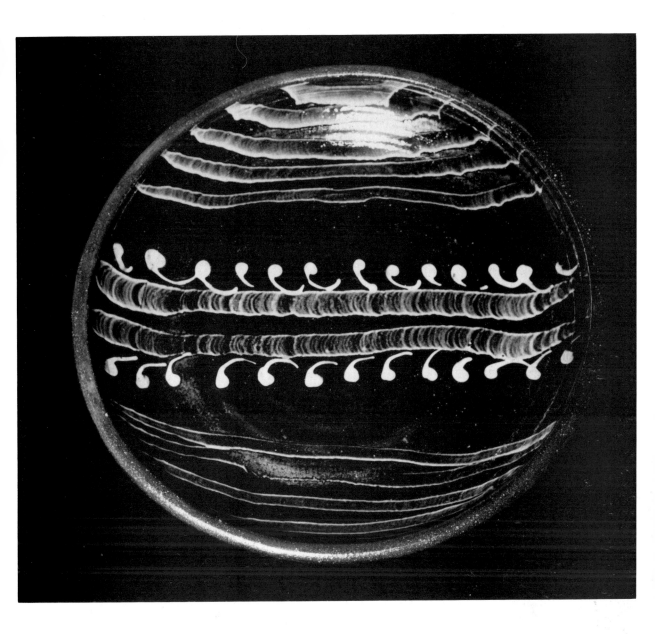

Clive Bowen
16.   Woodfired, earthenware plate, 56 cm diam. Black and white slip decoration.

Bill Brown
17. Porcelain plate. painted decoration.

Ian Byers
18. Opening form, raku.*
19. Balancing form, raku.

Alan Caiger-Smith
20. Large woodfired earthenware bowl, iron-brown, blue green and manganese brush decoration, tin glaze, black rim.*
21. Earthenware bowl, brush decoration, red lustre glaze.

Michael Casson
22. Large store jar, stoneware, inlaid porcellanous slip, wood ash glaze, oil-fired. 1280°C*
23. Handled bowl on feet, decoration as above.

Sheila Casson
24. Porcelain tall form. Decorated by combination of inlay, paper resist, sprayed
    slips, sgraffito. Dolomite and tin, gas fired 1280°C.*

Jenny Clarke
26. Large bowl, incised stoneware.

Derek Clarkson

27. Bottle. stoneware. wood ash glaze, cobalt and iron brushwork decoration.
28. Bottle. porcelain. wood ash glaze, cobalt and iron brushwork decoration.*
29. Bottle. stoneware. tenmoku glaze, ilmenite brush decoration.*

Margery Clinton
30. Bowl, 28 cm. diam, white tin glaze with reduction lustre glaze decoration.

Barbara Colls
31. Swallow, bird-lidded pot, porcelain.

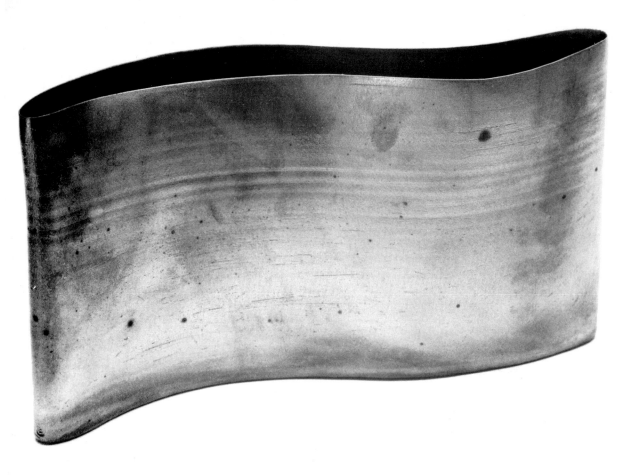

Joanna Constantinidis
32. Porcelain pot with lines, red/gold lustrous surface with dark lines.
33. Narrow curved stoneware pot, dark inside, lustrous red/gold outside.
34. Narrow curved stoneware pot, dark inside, lustrous red/gold outside.*

Delan Cookson
35. "Egg Press". Handbuilt stoneware and porcelain with glass assembled from slabbed and thrown sections.

Emmanuel Cooper
36. Bottle, porcelain, thrown, electric kiln 1260°C.
37. Bottle, porcelain, pink and grey glaze, thrown, electric kiln 1260°C.
38. Bowl, porcelain, spiral decoration, thrown, electric kiln 1260°C.*

Suzi Cree
39. Teapot, woodfired earthenware, slip decorated.

Dartington Pottery
40. Large serving dish, stoneware, shino glaze, brush decoration.

John Davidson
41.   Bowl, stoneware, decorated with blue/brown brushwork.

John Davies
42. Jug, hawthorn ash and granite glaze, with red trailed glaze over. Fired to cone 9, reduced.

Derek Davis
43.   Stoneware dish, fired to 1330°C.

Peter Dick
46. Large bowl with slip decoration, high-fired earthenware.*
47. Deep bowl, undecorated, high-fired earthenware.

Mike Dodd
48. Vase, crackled slip, stoneware.
49. Cut bowl, stoneware.*

Geoffrey Eastop
50. Earthenware dish, coloured glazes. "The Tree".
51. Segmented bottle with handle, porcelain.*

David Eeles
52. Vase, granite celadon glaze.
53. Vase, iron and celadon glaze, various pigments.*

Derek Emms
54. Stoneware teapot, tenmoku, rust decoration.*
55. Porcelain bowl, blue decoration.

Dorothy Feibleman
56. Lunar vessel, hand-built, agate ware porcelain.*
57. Pinched zig-zag vessel, hand-built, agate ware porcelain.
58. Turquoise, green and yellow, pierced zig-zag, hand-built, agate ware porcelain.

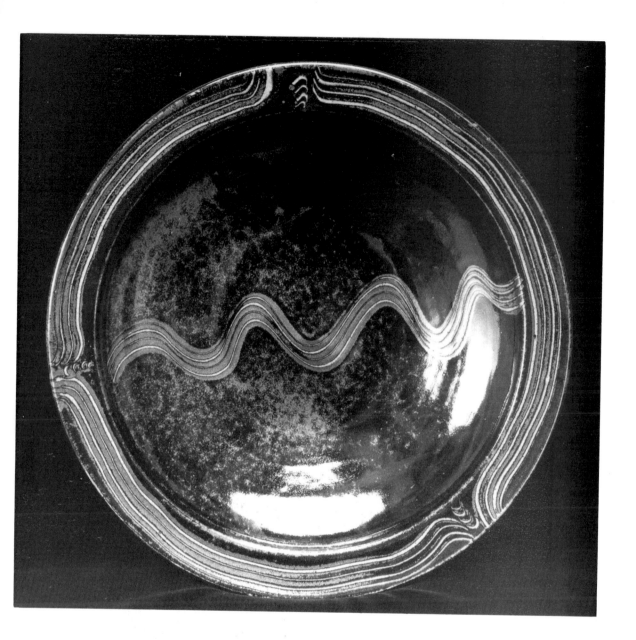

Ray Finch

59. Cider jar, 2 gallons, stoneware, finger-wipe decoration.
60. Teapot, stoneware, decoration incised through slip.
61. Large platter, stoneware, finger-wipe decoration.*

Robert Fournier
62. Black and gold, copper/manganese handbuilt bottle, stoneware.*
63. Black and gold, copper/manganese handbuilt bottle, stoneware.

Sheila Fournier
64.   Inlaid porcelain bowl.

Ruth Franklin
65.   Lady on Beach. 32 cm, earthenware clay, acrylic paint. 1100°C.

David Frith
66. Square dish, celadon glaze, wax decoration, blue wash, kaki trailing.
67. Beaten jar, green celadon kaki trailing, wax kaki overglaze.
68. Platter, green celadon, wax vine pattern, kaki overglaze.*

Annette Fuchs
69. Bowl, stoneware, oxidised.

Tessa Fuchs
70. Oak, red earthenware, oxidised.

Ian Gregory
71.   Teapot, salt-glazed stoneware.
72.   Basket, salt-glazed stoneware.*

Arthur Griffiths
73.   Porcelain dry glaze pot, reduced, 1280°C.*
74.   Ash glaze pot, porcelain, reduced, 1280°C.

Jane Hamlyn
75.   Saltglazed porcelain jug.*
76.   Saltglazed porcelain mug.
77.   Saltglazed porcelain mug.

Ewen Henderson
78. Laminated striped dish, handbuilt, stoneware, porcelain, bone china, oxidised, 1260°C.
79. Little squat bottle — as above.*
80. Jagged flared jar — as above.

Joan Hepworth
81.   Small carrier bag, cast porcelain, ceramic crayon decoration.

Anita Hoy
82. Bowl, stoneware, slip painted under blue celadon glaze.

John Huggins
83. Sun and rain tub, terracotta.*
84. Sun and rain pot, terracotta, 25.5 cm.

Neil Ions
85. Vase "Let me take you down", hand-built earthenware.
86. Harmonic flute (otter with garnets), hand-built earthenware.
87. Bird ocarina — African pygmy goose, hand-built earthenware.*

John Jelfs
88. Squared bottle, stoneware, celadon glaze, combed iron slip.*
89. Round bottle, stoneware, celadon glaze, combed iron slip.

Chris Jenkins
90.   Deep bowl, inlaid decoration, stoneware.*
91.   Shallow bowl with masked decoration, stoneware.

David Lloyd Jones
92.   Very large lidded jar, tenmoku glaze, stoneware.

Walter Keeler

93.   Teapot, saltglazed stoneware, wheel-thrown, altered and assembled.

94.   Jug, saltglazed stoneware, wheel-thrown, altered and assembled.

95.   Carafe, saltglazed stoneware, wheel-thrown and altered.*

Ruth King
96.   Large square bowl, grey with cream spots, hand-built stoneware.*
97.   Tall dark grey pot, hand-built stoneware.

Peter Lane
98. Porcelain bowl with carved and pierced rim, white crackled glaze.
99. Porcelain bowl with matt brown rim, white crackled glaze and gold lustre.*

David Leach

Janet Leach

103. Tall red clay pot, hamstone glaze, stoneware.
104. Slab pot, red clay, hamstone glaze, stoneware.
105. Wood fired pot, stoneware.*

John Leach
106. Large tall pitcher, wood fired stoneware.
107. Large cross-handled bottle — as above.*

Eileen Lewenstein
108. Porcelain bottle, brown/green mottle glaze.
109. Porcelain bottle, blue with poured glaze.*
110. "Wave Variations". Press moulded stoneware dish with slip decoration.

John Lomas
111. Wood ash glazed jug, combed decoration.

Andrew McGarva
112.   Painted mushroom dish, wood fired, raw glazed stoneware.

Mal Magson
113. Small footed bowl, hand-built agate stoneware and porcelain.*
114. Bottle — as above.

Jim Malone
115.   Coffee pot, stoneware, tenmoku glaze.

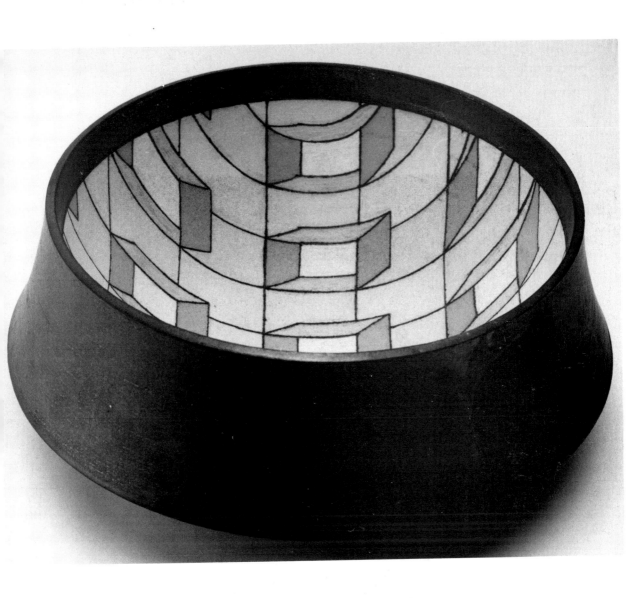

Peter Meanley
116. Slip decorated gold bowl featuring geometric perspective imagery, stoneware.

William Mehornay
117. Lemon yellow bowl, 18 cm. porcelain.
118. Cobalt blue bowl, porcelain.*

Eric Mellon
119. Bowl with painted decoration, stoneware, 1983.
120. Bulbous pot, with painted decoration, stoneware, 1982.*

David Miller
121. Vase, smoked raku.

David Morris
22. Square dish, stoneware, slab built.

Bryan Newman
123. Bridge, stoneware.
124. Boat, stoneware.*

Siddig El'Nigoumi
125. "Greenham Common", earthenware, burnished incised and smoked.
126. "The Great Royal Wedding" — as above.*

Eileen Nisbet
127. Porcelain sculpture.

Magdalene Odundo

128.   Symmetrical ribbed pot, burnished red clay, bisque 950 – 1000°C, reduction firing in saggars to 800°C.*

129.   Angled ribbed pot — as above

Warwick Parker
130. Handled dish with rocks at low tide, stoneware.

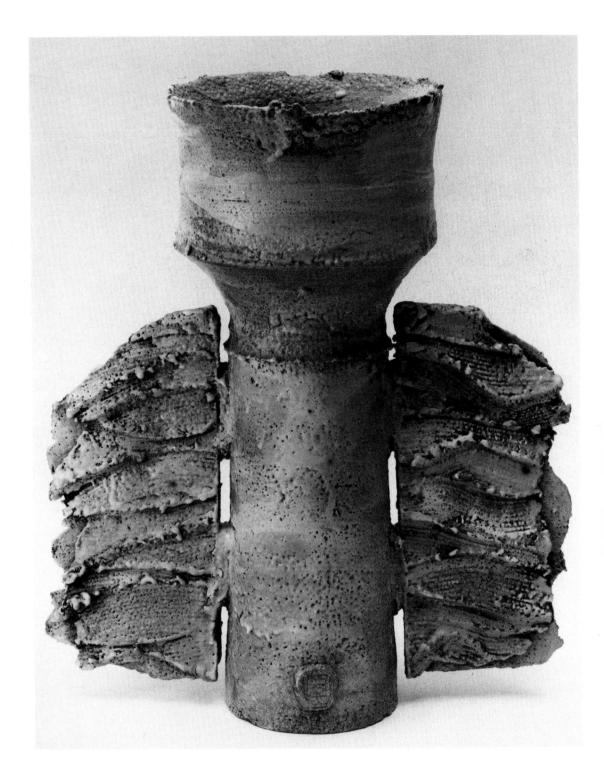

Colin Pearson
131. Winged stoneware vase, brushed coloured slips, combed and carved wings, semi-matt glazes, oxidised 1280°C.

Ian Pirie
132. Asymmetric plate, porcelain.*
133. Asymmetric assembled form, porcelain.

Katharine Pleydell-Bouverie
134. Stoneware pot, incised decoration, wood-ash glaze, oxidised.*
135. Bottle, stoneware, carved, wood-ash decoration, oxidised.

John Pollex
136.   Harvest jug, earthenware, slip-trailed and incised decoration.

Stanislas Reychan
137. "Bacchus", earthenware, majolica.

Christine-Ann Richards
138. Long necked peach bloom bottle, porcelain.*
139. Long necked stained white crackle bottle, porcelain.

Dave Roberts
140.   Coil built vessel, raku.

Mary Rogers
141. "Sliced Agate", hand-modelled porcelain.*
142. "Lotus", hand-modelled porcelain.
143. "Radiating Stripes", hand-modelled porcelain.

David Scott
144. Earthenware teapot.
145. Earthenware teapot, with plastic handle.*

Ray Silverman
146.   Oxidised porcelain bottle.

Peter Smith
147. Jug — earthenware, wheel-thrown and altered, coal fired.*
148. Bowl — earthenware, wheel-thrown and altered, coal fired.

John Solly
149   Small bottle, cobalt/iron wash under feldspathic tin glaze, incised.

Gary Standige
150. Blue bowl, stoneware, cut rim.*
151. Blue ellipse, stoneware.

Peter Starkey
152. Two lidded jars, saltglazed stoneware, blue slip.
153. Teapot, saltglazed stoneware, blue/tan slip.*

Peter Stoodley
154. Stoneware garden planter, incised decoration.

Harry Horlock Stringer
155.   Open bowl, cut decoration, stoneware.

Ielen Swain
56. Flowing vessel, red earthenware 1040°C. *Photograph by Frank Swain.*

Geoffrey Swindell

157.   Wheelmade porcelain pot.
158.   Wheelmade porcelain pot.
159.   Wheelmade porcelain pot.

Vera Tollow
160.   Vase, tenmoku glaze with iron and glaze decoration, stoneware.

Marianne de Trey
161.   Porcelain bowl, inlaid copper slip.

Alan Wallwork
162. Smooth boulder, stoneware.

Sarah Walton
163. Large bowl. saltglazed stoneware.*

John Ward
164. White handbuilt bowl with green banded design, stoneware.
165. Rounded brown, black and blue handbuilt bowl, stoneware.*

Robin Welch

166. Stoneware bowl with low-fired glaze.*
167. Stoneware vase with low-fired glaze.

Mary White
168.   Flanged dish, porcelain.

Geoffrey Whiting

169. Stoneware tenmoku bowl.
170. Stoneware "kettle" teapot.*

Caroline Whyman
171. Oval vase with ribs, porcelain.*
172. Oval vase with dots and ribs, porcelain.

Nigel Wood
173. Large stoneware fruitbowl, kaki glaze over ash glaze, finger combing and incised decoration. Fireclay to 1260°C.

Rosemary Wren
174. Standing Heron, stoneware.*
175. Lapwing, stoneware.

Takeshi Yasuda
176. Plate with twisted handles, stoneware.
177. Plate with twisted handles, stoneware.

Poh Chap Yeap
178. Porcelain polychrome bowl.*
179. Porcelain stem cup, crackle glaze.

Andrew & Joanna Young
180. Standard oval casserole, stoneware.
181. Eye shaped bowl on foot, gold inside, green glaze with small white sprigs, stoneware.
182. Eye shaped bowl, handled, dog-tooth and sprigged decoration, stoneware.*

Directory of CPA Members 1983

Pots in the Craftsmen Potters Shop

Upon election to full membership of the association, potters are entitled to send work of their choice to the shop on a sale or return basis. This work is looked at regularly by the selection committee (the full council plus shop manager) to ensure that craft standards are maintained. In addition the shop manager can, with council approval, purchase some work from members outright.

Adrian Abberley

Home:
50A Earls Court Square
London SW5
(01) 373 6161
Shop and Pottery:
Cabin Pottery
60A Golborne Road
London W10

Works alone making individual pieces and some domestic ware in oxidised stoneware and porcelain, using combination of slab built and thrown sections.

Showroom open Saturdays. At other times please phone.

Chris Aston

The Pottery
4 High Street
Elkesley
nr Retford
Nottinghamshire
DN22 8AY
Gamston 391
(STD code 077 783)

Full-time potter for 16 years, working in converted farm buildings with wife and one part-time assistant. Produces full range of domestic and individual work, mostly decorated with distinctive iron and copper red brushwork under either Cornish stone matt glaze or glossy celadon green. Porcelain produced in sang de boeuf or with carved celadon decoration. All pots made from filter pressed clay body to own recipe, and fired in 90 cu. ft. kerosene fuel kiln designed and built by himself. Individual commissions for Clubs, Colleges, Schools etc. also undertaken using ceramic motif technique. Leaflet on request.

Visitors welcome to workshop and showroom seven days a week 10am — 6pm. Wholesale and retail enquiries welcome.

Mick Arnup

Holtby Pottery
Holtby
York YO1 3UA
York 489377
(STD code 0904)

Makes a range of oil fired reduced stoneware including large decorated plates and dishes. Trained as painter at Kingston and Royal College with pottery always an important second interest. Resigned as Head of Fine Art at York in 1972 and built present workshop and showroom shared with his wife, the sculptor Sally Arnup, with whom he has exhibited both in the U.K. and abroad. Painting is still a commitment and important in the search for a personal method of pot decoration.

Showroom open 10.00 to 6.00 daily. (Holtby — A166 5 miles from York).

Gordon Baldwin

1 Willowbrook
Eton, Windsor
Berks
Windsor 65064
(STD code 075 35)

Hampton House
60 Shropshire Street
Market Drayton
Shropshire
Market Drayton 2737
(STD code 0630)

Works on individual pieces which are all signed and dated.

Visitors to studio welcome by appointment.

(Hampton House — Christmas and Easter periods and end of July — beginning of September)

**...th and Alan
...rrett-Danes**
...he Laurels"
...Chapel Road
...ergavenny
...ent
...ergavenny 4329
...TD code 0873)

Val Barry
86 Cecile Park London
N8 9AU
(01) 340 3007

B

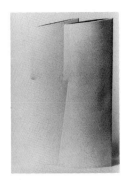

...dividual pieces worked around one main theme in limited ...itions. Work in high fired earthenware and porcelain ...ploying a variety of techniques including hand modelling, ...ess-moulding and throwing. Exhibit widely and work ...presented in museums and private collections in Britain and ...road. Ruth tutors at University Hospital of Wales. Alan is ...nior Lecturer in Ceramics at Cardiff College of Art.

...sitors by appointment only.

Studio established 1971. Sculptural potter. Abstract sculptural pieces, handbuilt in stoneware and semi porcelain clay. Exhibited widely in this country and abroad, including The Craftmens Art, Victoria and Albert Museum; Syracuse Museum, New York; Zurich; Faenza; British Council Exhibition, Hong Kong. Work sold through Craft Shop, Victoria and Albert Museum; Oxford Gallery; Peter Dingley; Bohun Gallery. Work represented in many public collections including Victoria and Albert Museum, Manchester City Art Gallery, Auckland Museum, New Zealand. Gold Medal International Ceramics Exhibition Faenza 1975, 2nd Prize Bendigo Internaional Ceramics Exhibition Australia 1976.

Visitors by appointment. Not possible to take assistants.

...aul Barron
...hornfield
...entley
...rnham, Surrey
...entley 22209
...TD code 0420)

Svend Bayer
Duckpool Cottage
Sheepwash
Beaworthy
North Devon
Beaworthy 282
(STD Code 040 922)

...ome series pieces but mainly one-off reduced stoneware using ...ood ash and local minerals in the glazes and firing with gas. ...tarted potting at Brighton School of Art in 1937 and later at the ...oyal College of Art. Joined Henry Hammond at Farnham School ...f Art in 1950 and helped to build what is now BA(Hons) ...eramics, West Surrey College of Art. Now retired. Established ...ie studio, a converted hop-kiln at Bentley in 1953 and has ...orked there spasmodically ever since. Exhibited in many ...ational and Society exhibitions and Takashimaya Store, Tokyo ...1971. Represented in Victoria and Albert Museum and in ...veral provincial museums.

...isitors by apointment only. It is not possible to employ assistants ...r trainees at present.

Garden Pots and reduced stoneware.

Michael Bayley
Beechcroft Cottage
Green Lane
Temple Ewell
Dover, Kent CT16 3AS
Dover 822624
(STD code 0304)

Pressmoulded bowls, hand-built pots and wall-hangings in oxidised stoneware and porcelain. Use of agate and inlay techniques. Mostly unglazed. Trained at Hornsey College of Art. Exhibited at home and abroad.

Visitors welcome by appointment.

Terry Bell-Hughes
'Fron Dirion'
Conway Road
Llandudno Junction
Gwynedd
Deganwy 82912
(STD code 0492)

Reduced and oxidised stoneware, thrown and hand built. Born 1939. Studied at teacher training college Barry and Harrow School of Art. Teaches two days at Sutton Liberal Arts College. Exhibited in various exhibitions at home and abroad.

Visitors welcome by appointment.

Peter Beard
The Pottery
Bottom Ponds Road
Wormshill
Nr Sittingbourne
Kent ME9 0TR
Wormshill 554
(STD code 062 784)

Born 1951. Studied Ravensbourne College of Art 1970-73. Started workshop 1974. Works alone making individual pieces made mainly in reduced stoneware and porcelain. Work at present generally incorporates porcelain 'mushroom' forms with matt black geometric and thrown pieces. Prices from £3-£100. Work sold throughout the country and abroad.

Visitors welcome to the studio, but only by appointment.

Tony Benham
Preston House
Preston
Nr Canterbury
Kent CT3 1DZ
Preston 324
(STD code 022 73)

Started potting at Wimbledon School of Art in 1951. Worked at Wateringbury Mill from 1965-78. Now at Preston near Canterbury making gas fired pots, with Maureen Duck. Does not take students.

Workshop not open to the public. Visitors by previous appointment.

**Maggie Angus
Berkowitz**
1/23 Park Road
Milnthorpe
Cumbria
Milnthorpe 3970
(STD code 044 82)

Individual pictorial panels of glazed earthenware or vitrified tiles.
Designs are worked in glaze, poured, trailed, cut and filled,
rather than painted. Has worked, studied and taught in schools
and workshops in UK, Tanzania, Italy (Faenza) and USA. Likes
to discuss work for particular settings with commissioning clients.
Prices from £60 for a panel of four tiles. Works alone.

Prospective clients by appointment.

Clive Bowen
Shebbear Pottery
Shebbear
Beaworthy
Devon EX21 5QZ
Shebbear 271
(STD code 040 928)

The pottery was established in 1971. The pots are thrown in red
earthenware clay and range from large scale store jars and garden
pots to mugs and eggs cups. The domestic ware and one-off pots
may be decorated with three contrasting slips, using slip trailing,
combing and sgraffito methods. The pots are once-fired in a
round (8' dia.) down-draught wood-fired kiln to 1040°C-1060°C
(less for garden pots).

Wholesale and retail customers are welcome at the showroom.

Audrey Blackman
Wood Croft
Foxcombe Lane
Boars Hill
Oxford OX1 5DH
Oxford 735148
(STD code 0865)

Works with porcelain bisque with marbled, inlaid and impressed
decoration using stained clay in many colours. The technique is
described in 'Rolled Pottery Figures' by Audrey Blackman
(Pitman) and in German (Hornemann Verlag of Bonn). Work
can be seen at the Fitzwilliam Museum, Cambridge; City of
Stoke-on-Trent Museum; the Paisley Museum; Cecil Higgins
Museum, Bedford; the Oxford City and County Museum; the
Crafts Study Centre at the Holburne Museum in Bath. Stoneware
and stained glass sculpture in the Pilkington Glass Museum, St.
Helens, Lancs. Work on sale at the above address. Single figures
£95, groups from £120. Each work is signed 'A. Blackman', dated
and numbered.

Visitors welcome by appointment.

Bill Brown
Monyroads
Monymusk
Inverurie
Aberdeen
Scotland
Monymusk 375 or 219
(STD code 046 77)

Produces individual pieces of stoneware and porcelain as well as
domestic stoneware and some cast earthenware. Trained at Grays
School of Art, Aberdeen, from 1969 to 1974. Began potting on
leaving college. At present workshop since 1979. Work exhibited
widely throughout the country and occasionally abroad.

Showroom (at 14 The Square, Monymusk) open 10-5 Thursday —
Monday. Visitors welcome at the workshop at any reasonable
time, but it is advisable to telephone first.

Graham Burr
7 Egerton Drive
Greenwich
London SE10
(01) 692 2634

Sculpture and occasional painted bowls. Trained at Chelmsford
and Camberwell Art Schools. Senior Lecturer at Ravensbourne
College of Art. Exhibits widely in U.K. and abroad.

Visitors by appointment.

Alan Caiger-Smith
Aldermaston Pottery
Aldermaston Village
Berkshire RG7 4LW
Woolhampton 3359
(STD code 073 521)

Works with six assistants producing a wide range of decorated tin-
glaze earthenware, mostly brush-painted and much of it wood-
fired. Tableware includes mugs, goblets, bowls, plates, ovenware
etc. Also ceremonial pieces and commissions and smoked lustres.

Visitors welcome to showroom by appointment 8am — 5pm
except Tuesdays and Sundays.

Ian Byers
10 Westbourne Road
Croydon
Surrey CR0 6HP
(01) 654 0225

Most of the early pieces in Raku were influenced by the colour
and pattern of certain textile traditions. "I like to take a pattern
apart, put it together again in a different form or transpose it to
another pattern all on the same piece. I have been interested in
making every part of the pot speak and I work over every last bit
of the surface. Edges and feet can be beginnings or ends, or a
pause, a contrast a link between surfaces inside and out, upside
and down. My aims for the future must include experiencing,
questioning and enjoying".

I have no showroom but work sold from studio.

Barbara Cass
The Arden Pottery
31 Henley Street
Stratford-on-Avon
Warwickshire

Studied sculpture in Berlin. Self taught potter. Different wood
ash glazes produce colourful stoneware pots fired in reduction in
a gas kiln. Mostly individual pieces. Two one-potter shows in
London, exhibits widely in this country and abroad. Work
included in the Victoria and Albert Museum, numerous other art
galleries and in private collections. No students taken at present.
Sells at own showroom.

Visitors welcome.

Michael Casson
Wobage Farm
Upton Bishop
Ross-on-Wye
Herefordshire
Upton Bishop 233
(STD code 098 985)

Producing mainly individual decorated pieces, all thrown. Oil fired, wood fired and wood fired saltglazed stoneware and porcelain..

Showroom open at all reasonable times. Visitors to workshops please telephone first.

Jenny Clarke
25 Etloe Road
Westbury Park
Bristol BS6 7NZ
Bristol 735193
(STD code 0272)

Trained at Farnham School of Art. Works alone, producing a range of domestic stoneware, and some individual porcelain pots.

Visitors welcome by appointment.

Sheila Casson
Wobage Farm
Upton Bishop
Ross-on-Wye
Herefordshire
HR9 7QP
Upton Bishop 233
(STD code 098 985)

Started potting in 1947. Since 1967 has concentrated on making thrown individual porcelain bowls and tall vases with decoration inspired by the South Herefordshire landscape. The decoration is accomplished by a combination of inlaying and spraying coloured slips with paper resist and sgraffito. Dolomite and tin glaze reduction fired in a gas kiln to 1280°C.

Showroom open at all reasonable times. Visitors to workshops please telephone first.

Derek Clarkson
1 The Poplars
Bacup
Lancs OL13 8AD
Bacup 874541
(STD code 0706)

Works alone making individual pieces in reduced stoneware and porcelain, 1300°C. Thrown and turned bottle forms major preoccupation. Smooth waxy cream wood ash glaze with iron: iron/cobalt brush decoration often used, or wax resist and double glaze technique using ash, kaki, celadon and tenmoku glazes. Titanium aventurine glaze and copper reds used without further decoration. Exhibitions national and international, represented in public and private collections. Prices from £3. Enjoys giving lectures/demonstrations. Does not take students.

Visitors to workshop and display of work welcome at any reasonable time.

Margery Clinton

The Pottery
Newton Port
Haddington
East Lothian
Haddington 3584
(STD code 062 082)

Trained as a painter at Glasgow School of Art. Began working in ceramics in the early sixties. Has specialised in reduction lustres since beginning research at the Royal College of Art in 1973. Casts goblets, boxes and cylinder vases as well as making individual pieces. Moved from London to Haddington in 1978 to establish the pottery. Works with two part-time assistants. Work in various public and private collections including Victoria and Albert Museum and HRH Duke of Edinburgh.

Showroom open Tuesday to Saturday 10—1 and 2.30—5.30. Workshop open on Saturday mornings and by appointment.

Russell Collins

The Pottery
East End Farm House
Hook Norton
Oxon
Hook Norton 737414
(STD code 0608)

A large range of domestic stoneware produced in a double chamber, oil-fired kiln. There are also many indivdual pieces made, mostly large bowls and jars as well as some porcelain. A team of five people are employed and the kiln is fired weekly.

The Showroom displays a varied selection of work and is open 9.30 to 5.30 Monday to Saturday.

Michael Cole

Corlwyni Pottery
Nantmor
Caernarvon
Gwynedd, Wales
Beddgelert 331
(STD code 076 686)

Been making pottery for 15 years. Works alone. Was apprenticed to Colin Pearson before establishing present pottery in a farmhouse in North Wales in 1966. The clay and glazes are made up from raw materials, using a red Dorset clay for the body. Glazes used are a tenmoku and grey matt with a variety of ash glazes including a chun. Ware is raw glazed and once fired by oil and gas in a 21 cubic feet down-draft kiln to 1260°C in a reduced atmosphere. Produces domestic stoneware and some sculptural work. Main outlets local craft shops and the pottery, a twenty minute walk from the road.

Visitors: Showroom/workshop 9.00 — 6.00 weekdays.

Barbara Colls

177 Thunder Lane
Thorpe St. Andrew
Norwich NR7 0JF
Norwich 36695
(STD code 0603)

Oxidised stoneware and porcelain bird-lidded pots mostly oven proof. Trained Norwich School of Art and part-time at West Surrey College of Art and Design. Exhibitions at Guildford House, Black Horse Craft Centre, Norwich and at many galleries abroad.

Visitors welcome by appointment.

Joanna Constantinidis

2 Bells Chase
Great Baddow
Chelmsford
Essex CM2 8DT
*Chelmsford 71842
(STD code 0245)*

Stoneware and procelain. Individual pieces. Wheel-made usually reduction fired in a gas kiln. Exhibited widely in this country and abroad. Full-time Lecturer in charge pottery department. Chelmer Institute of Higher Education. Works alone, no students. Some sales direct to public.

Visitors by appointment only.

Emmanuel Cooper

Fonthill Pottery
38 Chalcot Road
London NW1 8LS
(01) 722 9090

Makes range of domestic stoneware and individual pots which include bowls and boxes, mostly with matt glazes fired in electric kiln. Has been potting for 20 years. Exhibited widely in great Britain and abroad. Work in Victoria and Albert Museum collection. Co-editor of *Ceramic Review*. Author of many books including 'New Ceramics' (with Eileen Lewenstein) (Studio Vista 1974) 'Pottery' (Macdonald Educational) 'Glazes for the Studio Potter' with Derek Royle (Batsford 1978) 'Glaze Recipes' (Batsford 1980) 'A History of World Pottery' (Batsford 1980).

Visitors welcome by appointment. Monday to Saturday 10-5.

Delan Cookson

Little Paddock
33A Green Lane
Radnage, Bucks.
*Radnage 3714
(STD code 024 026)*

Small editions of decorative pots and individual pieces of sculptural ceramics. Born 1937, trained at Bournemouth and Central School. Exhibitions include: Oxford Gallery 1974, Whitworth Gallery 1977, CPA 1978, Phoenix Gallery 1981, Cologne 1983. Awarded gold medal at Vallauris Internatinal Exhibition of Ceramics 1974.

Visitors welcome by appointment.

Suzi Cree

Folly Gill Mill
Thornthwaite
Harrogate
North Yorkshire
HG3 2QU
*Harrogate 780095
(STD code 0423)*

Makes functional, thrown, once-fired earthenware, fired in a wood kiln, exploiting traditional techniques — commissions welcomed. Trained at Harrow School of Art, established present workshop in 1979. Teaches part-time at Harrogate College of Art.

Visitors by appointment.

Peter M. Crotty
The Oxshott Pottery
Mill Cottage
Lustleigh
Newton Abbot
Devon
Lustleigh 231
(STD code 064 77)

John Davidson
New Mills Pottery
New Mills
Ladock
Truro
Cornwall TR2 4NN
St. Austell 882209
(STD code 0726)

Works in partnership with Rosemary Wren and they both work on each piece produced. His responsibility is decoration and firing of the work. The patterned surface of each creature is divided into 'compartments' which are individually filled in by brushwork. This technique enables a controlled use to be made of sharp contrasts — say cobalt black beside tin white, even under a reducing atmosphere at stoneware temperatures. Prices £10 -£350.

The workshop is now at Lustleigh — 1 mile off the Bovey Tracey/Moretonhampstead Road (A386) and being accessible, visitors are welcome. Please telephone first.

A comprehensive range of domestic stoneware, mostly decorated in blue on a grey/celadon glaze. More recently a variety of individual pieces including lustre decoration on porcelain. Largely self taught after a good basic introduction by Harry Stringer. Currently working alone, using self-built oil-fired kiln.

Visitors are welcome. Showroom on premises.

Dartington Pottery
Training Workshop
Shinners Bridge
Dartington
Totnes
Devon TQ9 6JE
Totnes 864163
(STD code 0803)

Clive Davies
The Pottery
Withersdale
Harleston
Norfolk IP20 0JG
Fressingfield 407
(STD code 037 986)

Wide range of domestic stoneware, most of which is decorated, with some porcelain and individual pieces, such as large platters, bread bins, pitchers and vases. Pots are fired in a 60 cu.ft. oil-fired down-draught kiln every few weeks. Workshop at present run by Peter Cook and Stephen Course together with five trainees who stay for periods ranging from eighteen months to two years depending on previous experience.

Visitors welcome any time but please telephone first.

Produces domestic and individual stoneware with a variety of glazes.

Visitors very welcome but please telephone first as opening times somewhat erratic.

John Davies
Gwynedd Pottery
Y Ffor (Fourcrosses)
Pwllheli
Wales LL53 6RR
Pwllheli 612932
(STD code 0758)

Crochendy
Gwynedd,
Pwllheli

Sally Dawson
2 Albion Square
London E8 4ES
(01) 249 0760

Mainly individual pieces and a small range of purely domestic items, all thrown. Decorated with applied slips, glaze-over-glaze and engraving under glazes, using much locally gathered raw materials. Self-taught. Began making pottery in 1956. Started present workshop in 1966. Works alone with two kilns, one is LPG fuelled and the other with wood. Work is always on sale direct from the pottery. Wholesale orders are also gladly undertaken for shops and galleries. Enquiries from EEC countries are welcome. Illustrations and price guides are available on request.

Callers are welcome at our showroom, which is open nearly every day, all year round, but it is best to write or telephone prior to calling.

Works alone producing mostly porcelain. Self taught.

Visitors by appointment.

Derek Davis
Duff House
Maltravers Street
Arundel, Sussex.
Arundel 882600
(STD code 0903)
Showroom:
Duff Gallery
Tarrant Street
Arundel

Davis

Peter B. Dick
Coxwold Pottery
Coxwold
York YO6 4AA
Coxwold 344
(STD code 034 76)

Individual pieces in stoneware and procelain. Decorative and functional ware fired 1320°C-1350°C. Trained in painting Central School, London. Exhibitions include Liberty, Amalgam, Peter Dingley, Primavera, also USA, Europe, Turkey and Japan. Collections include Garth Clark USA. Artist in Residence University of Sussex 1967. Chosen by Dr. Roy Strong (V & A) with Mary Rogers for 'The Spirit of the Seventies' Sunday Times 1976. Ceramics shown on Japanese TV Network 1982. Member of The International Academy of Ceramics.

Showroom open to public most days.

Works with two assistants making useful pots of all types in earthenware and stoneware. Most pots are made on the wheel and decorated with slip or by impressing patterns. Wood and waste oil are used to fire the three chambered kiln (on average 8 times a year). Trained by Michael Cardew and Ray Finch.

Showroom open 10.00 — 5.00 weekdays and visitors are welcome to see the workshop when convenient. Telephone prior to weekend or group visits.

Mike Dodd
Wellrash
Boltongate
Wigton
Cumbria
Wigton 28139
(STD code 0228)

Geoffrey Eastop
Fawley Pottery
Fawley Bottom
Farmhouse,
Nr. Henley-on-Thames
Oxon
Telephone evenings
Reading 332598
(STD code 0734)

Presently establishing a pottery course (DATEC) at Cumbria College of Art and Design. The intention of this course is to provide a space for students to develop their own inner resources in the context of sound craftmanship with a view to setting up their own workshops. "Personally I am making pots mainly for exhibition. Half the profits from any exhibition will go to the 'Hunger Project', an organization of people committed to ending world hunger in the year 2000".

Work is directed mainly towards production of individual pieces in porcelain and stoneware, and large earthenware dishes in coloured glazes.

Visitors welcome by appointment.

Micky Doherty
Mewith Pottery
Bentham
Nr. Lancaster
Bentham 61461
(STD code 0468)

David Edmonds
45 Devonshire Drive
Greenwich
London SE10
(01) 692 8964

Makes a wide range of tableware, including bread crocks with wooden lids, large salad bowls, teapots and tea bowls, tea caddies and hill jars. Has a 75 cu. ft. wood kiln in which to fire the pots raw. Likes to use simple clay slips and an ash glaze. The salting and the wood firing produce a wide range of colours, pinks, reds, blues and greys.

Showroom open 10am — 6pm. Visitors welcome throughout the year. Also wholesale.

"My pottery workshop is based at home in Greenwich where I have a one-man studio with wheel and 2 stoneware kilns. My work is mainly slab built, architectural in nature and decorated with birds and animals. I am engaged at present in experimenting with different clays, glazes and varying types of finish. I use mainly ash glazes which are fired to stoneware temperature".

I welcome visitors to my studio but a telephone appointment is most useful.

David Eeles
Shepherds's Well
Pottery
Mosterton
Beaminster
Dorset
Broadwindsor 8257
(STD code 030 86)

Derek Emms
Mossfield Cottage
Hayes Bank
Stone
Staffs
Stone 812048
(STD code 078 583)

Showrooms at Mosterton, and The Pot shop, 18 Barrack Street, Bridport. Dorset. The Pot Shop, A303, Watergore, Somerset. The Pot Shop, 56 Broad Street, Lyme Regis, Dorset. Showing the range of stoneware and porcelain which includes ovenware, tableware and lamps, cider and wine jars, platters and small and large individual pieces, made by David, Benjamin, Simon and Caroline Eeles.

Reduced stoneware and porcelain. Functional ware and individual pieces with painted or impressed decoration. Trained at Burnley and Leeds College of Art and at the Leach Pottery, St. Ives. Senior Lecturer, Department of 3 Dimensional Design (Ceramics) North Staffs Polytechnic in charge of the studio pottery section. Council member of the Red Rose Guild of Craftsmen.

Siddig El'Nigoumi
Mill House
Hatch Mill
Farnham
Surrey
Farnham 722844
(STD code 0252)

Miguel Espinosa
15 Mount Street
Cromer
Norfolk NR27 9DB

Studied general arts and crafts at Khartoum Art School and ceramics at the Central School of Art, London. Worked as Arabic Calligrapher at the Publications Bureau, Khartoum. At the moment the work consists mainly of individual burnished and decorated earthenware pots and dishes etc. Work exhibited widely in the UK including 'International Ceramics 1972' at the Victoria and Albert Museum. And abroad including 'Ceramic International' Faenza 1972 and 1975. And recently in Hong Kong. Amsterdam and Rotterdam. Work in many national and international collections. Teaches part-time at West Surrey College of Art and Design, Farnham, and block teaching at Medway College of Design, Rochester, Kent.

Works alone producing a wide range of domestic and decorative items in stoneware and porcelain, decorated with under glaze colours, fired in a gas kiln at 1270°C in reduced atmosphere.

Showroom open to public all the year round 10-6.30 (no telephone at the moment)

Visitors welcome by appointment.

Dorothy Feibleman
10 Arlingford Road
London SW2
(01) 674 8979

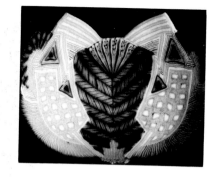

She has developed a technique which involves the lamination of coloured clays, usually porcelain. This 'marquetry ware' is often used in conjunction with other materials including precious metals, embroidery and feathers. She received a B.F.A. at the School for American Craftsmen, Rochester, New York, before setting up her first workshop in England in 1974. She has received numerous awards since 1971 in national shows in the U.S. for her inlaid porcelain jewellery and porcelain pieces. She undertakes commisions directly but sells also through galleries and exhibitions in England and abroad.

Robert Fournier
Fournier Pottery
(Robert and Sheila
Fournier)
The Tanyard, Lacock
Chippenham
Wiltshire
Lacock 266
(STD code 024 973)

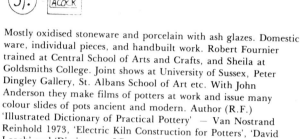

Mostly oxidised stoneware and porcelain with ash glazes. Domestic ware, individual pieces, and handbuilt work. Robert Fournier trained at Central School of Arts and Crafts, and Sheila at Goldsmiths College. Joint shows at University of Sussex, Peter Dingley Gallery, St. Albans School of Art etc. With John Anderson they make films of potters at work and issue many colour slides of pots ancient and modern. Author (R.F.) 'Illustrated Dictionary of Practical Pottery' — Van Nostrand Reinhold 1973, 'Electric Kiln Construction for Potters', 'David Leach' and 'Dictionary of Pottery Form' 1982.

Visitors welcome. Showroom open when working. Telephone call advisable in winter.

Ray Finch
Winchcombe Pottery
Winchcombe
Nr Cheltenham
Glos. GL54 5NU
Winchcombe 602462
(STD code 0242)

Works with six assistants. Wood fired domestic stoneware. Prices (standard range) from £1 to £30. Some individual pieces. Regret no places for students in the foreseeable future.

Visitors welcome at retail shop and (usually) workshop. Monday to Friday 9.00 - 5.00 Saturday 9.00 - 1.00. Please note definitely closed on Saturday afternoon and all day Sunday.

Sylvia Des Fours
The Pottery
Heather Hill
The Downs
Givons Grove
Leatherhead
Surrey
Leatherhead 72473
(STD code 037 23)

Thrown mainly domestic stoneware. Born in Czechoslovakia. Trained at Epsom School of Art and Hammersmith College of Art. Exhibits with the Dorking Group of Artists and Sussex Group of Artists. Teaches Adult Classes and works in two hospitals as art therapist.

Visitors welcome at workshop by appointment.

Ruth Franklin
Barbican Arts Group
Sycamore Street
London EC1Y 0SR
(01) 603 7284

R. FRANKLIN

"I make sculptural pieces in clay, and incorporate wood, metal, paper and found objects. I fire the clay once to 1100°C and then paint the unglazed pieces with acrylic paint. My work is figurative; mainly derived from drawings I make of people".

David Frith
Brookhouse Pottery
The Malt House
Brookhouse Lane
Denbigh
Clwyd, N. Wales
Denbigh 2805
(STD code 074 571)

Works with wife and one assistant. Started workshop 1963 after leaving Stoke on Trent College of Art. Produces range of hand-thrown domestic stoneware and a large selection of individual pieces. Work is decorated using ashes, Kaki, celadons, tenmokus and wax resist brushwork with overglazing and brushed pigments. Work is fired in down draught gas kiln and sold through craft shops in England, Wales and Germany. Member of the Craft Committee of the Welsh Arts Council. Lectures two days North Staffordshire Polytechnic.

Visitors welcome to the workshop. Showrooms open 9-6pm six days. Sundays — please ring before coming.

Alan Frewin
Mill House Pottery
1 Station Road
Harleston
Norfolk
Harleston 852556
(STD code 0379)

Produces a wide range of domestic ware, mainly once fired traditional slip-ware fired in a 120 cu.fit. natural gas kiln. Now in production a very comprehensive range of garden pots employing many decorative techniques. Apart from one week's tuition from John Shelly is self-taught. In 1965 having built a power-wheel and kiln he left engineering and began fulltime potting in London. In 1970 moved to Norfolk/Suffolk border to his present workshop. Exhibited in the Chagford Gallery, Devon 1969, Bedford Arts Centre 1972, Aldringham Craft Market 1975, Colchester Castle Museum 1976. Works with assistance from wife Ann and does not employ any other help. Sells retail and wholesale from showroom.

Visitors wishing to see workshop should make appointment.

Annette Fuchs
The Old School House
Witheridge Hill
Nr Henley-on-Thames
Oxon RG9 5PF
Nettlebed 641427
(STD code 0491)

Earthenware, stoneware and porcelain domestic ware and individual pieces. Trained at Royal Salford Technical College School of Art and Camberwell School of Art. Works alone. Has exhibited widely.

Visitors welcome by appointment only.

Tessa Fuchs
Home: 24 Cross Road
Kingston upon Thames
Surrey
(01) 549 6906
Studio:
26B Dunstable Road
Richmond
Surrey
(01) 940 1874

Ray Gardiner
77 Grandison Road
London SW11 6LT
(01) 228 9153

Sculptural pieces and practical ware with colourful glazes both matt and glossy. Trained Royal Salford Technical College Art School and Central School of Arts and Crafts. Works alone. Work shown in 'International Ceramics' and 'The Craftsman's Art' exhibitions at the Victoria and Albert Museum, and was one of seven potters taking part in 'New Ceramics' which travelled round Ireland. One-person shows: Sutton Liberal College of Arts, Commonwealth Institute, Southampton University, Boadicea, The Oxford Gallery. Featured as the potter in the BBC TV film 'In the making' shown in 1978 and 1979.

Visitors welcome by appointment.

Individual painted pieces in oxidised and reduced stoneware.

Sorry no visitors.

Tony Gant
53 Southdean Gardens
Southfields
London SW19 6NT
(01) 789 4518

Ian Godfrey
24 Holmsdale Road
London N 6

One man studio established in 1961, producing decorative and domestic stoneware. Trade enquiries only.

Individual stoneware pieces

reen Dene Pottery
reendene Croft
st Horsley
rrey
st Horsley 2668
TD code 048 65)

Arthur Griffiths
The White House
Walton-on-Wolds
Loughborough
Leics.
Wymeswold 880637
(STD code 0509)

udio pots in stoneware using particularly copper red and purple
azes and iron and ash glazes. Wood and oil fired kiln. Michael
uckland has worked in the pottery for 20 years. His pots were
cluded in the exhibition The Craftsman's Art' Victoria and
bert Museum 1973.

isitors welcome by appointment at workshop and showroom
.00 — 5.00 showroom only, weekends.

Individual and domestic stoneware and porcelain by oil fired
reduction. Worked with Harry Davis and The Leach Pottery prior
to taking charge of ceramics at Loughborough College of Art
1954-83. Work in private and public collections.

No showroom. Visitors by appointment.

n Gregory
he Pottery
nsty, Nr Dorchester
orset DT2 7PN
ilton Abbas 880891
TD code 0258)

Frank Hamer
Llwyn-on
Croes-yn-y-Pant
Mamhilad, Pontypool
Gwent NP4 8RE
Little Mill 282
(STD code 049 528)

ull range of domestic stoneware and saltglaze, including one-off
ems. Self-taught, workshop opened 1972. Exhibited both in
ritain and abroad.

isitors welcome 9 am to 5 pm Monday to Saturday.

Reduced stoneware includes goblets, loving cups, mugs, wall
plates and presentation pieces. Visiting lecturer, researcher and
writer. Runs courses. Founder member South Wales Potters
Association.

Visitors welcome preferably by appointment.

Jane Hamlyn
Millfield Pottery
Everton
Nr Doncaster
South Yorkshire
Retford 723
(STD code 0777 817)

Muriel Harris
La Fontenelle
Samares Lane
St. Clement
Jersey
Channel Islands
Jersey Central 54226
(STD code 0534)

Trained at Harrow School of Art, Studio Pottery course 1972-4. Works with husband, producing wide range of useful and decorative pots. All production is once fired saltglazed stoneware and porcelain. Oil-fired 60 cu.ft. kiln fired every 3-4 weeks. Most pots sold direct to shops from stock.

Visitors welcome at any reasonable time.

Makes individual pieces, fireplaces and some table and ovenware, all in stoneware. Works alone two miles from St. Helier and is glad to see visitors to her workshop by telephone appointment. Has been potting since 1946 and exporting to Dallas, New York and New Zealand. Shows in the island galleries, but direct sales to callers if desired.

Henry Hammond
St Maixent
Long Garden Walk
Farnham, Surrey
GU9 7HX
Farnham 714584
(STD code 0252)

Alan Heaps
Minhafren
Aberbechan
Newtown, Powys
Abermule 644
(STD code 068 686)

Studio at the Oast Pottery, Bentley shared with Paul Barron. Range of work includes reduced stoneware with brush decoration and slipware. Studied with W. Staite Murray at the Royal College of Art, Bernard Leach and Michael Cardew on his Geology for Potters Summer School. Exhibited at the Brygos Gallery. Primavera, CPA. Occasional Lectures and Demonstrations undertaken.

At present unable to take students at the studio.

Fantasy is an important element in his ceramics. Forms reflect interest in architecture, nature, mechanical objects and other cultures. Sees himself primarily as a designer using the qualities of clay to express ideas. All pieces are non-domestic one-offs, though the teapots can be used if you must. Work is built from thin slabs, carved and painted with coloured slip and usually using tin/barium glazes fired in an oxidising atmosphere. Theme of late include gardens for succulents, whistles, matchboxes, clocks and wheeled animals.

Visitors by appointment.

Ewen Henderson
Cliff Road
London NW1
(01) 485 5305

Nicholas Homoky
10 Bayswater Avenue
Westbury Park
Bristol BS6 7NS
Bristol 48255
(STD code 0272)

Assemblages of differing clays i.e. stoneware and porcelain coloured with oxides and stains put together in various ways so that the decoration and the pot are the same thing. Motifs used vary from stripes to spirals which after putting together are manipulated into forms relating as naturally as can to the decoration. All are oxidised stoneware covered with simple wood ash or Shino-type glazes mostly applied in raw state by brushing or similar methods.

No visitors.

Has worked mainly in porcelain, now also working with handbuilt stoneware and earthenware. Sells mainly through CPA, Beaux Arts, York Street, Bath, Oxford Gallery, British Crafts Centre and Victoria and Albert Museum Craft Shop.

Joan Hepworth
'Robin Cottage'
Stones Lane
Westcott, nr Dorking
Surrey
Dorking 880392
(STD code 0306)

J. Hepworth

Thomas Howard
21 Connaught Avenue
Loughton
Essex
IG10 4DS
(01) 508 6172

Slab and coiled individual pieces in stoneware also recently making slip cast porcelain pots. Studied design at Hastings School of Art. Won Royal Exhibition to Royal College of Art where also studied design. After working in a craft studio and on film cartoons began teaching at Sutton School of Art. When pottery was introduced to the school she joined a class and trained under Harry Horlock Stringer and Brian Starkey. Prices vary from £5 to £70.

Visitors welcome by appointment.

Individual thrown oxidised stoneware and porcelain for use rather than ornament. Range of about a dozen standard glazes. Occasional incised decoration and sometimes slip inlay decoration. 1953-1958 studied at local community association evening classes. Graduated as chemist from Cambridge. Works for pleasure not profit as potting is a spare time hobby.

Visitors by arrangement in limited numbers only.

Anita Hoy
50 Julian Avenue
London W3
(01) 992 4041

Neil Ions
Kitebrook Workshop
Home Farm
Kitebrook
Moreton-in-Marsh
Glos GL56 0RW
*Moreton-in-Marsh
74482
(STD Code 0608)*

Mainly individual pieces, earthenware, stoneware, porcelain. Working alone. Trained at Copenhagen College of Art. Started and became head of studio departments at Bullers Ltd., Stoke on Trent, and Royal Doulton at Lambeth, working with porcelain and saltglazed stoneware. Represented at Victoria and Albert Museum, and Stoke on Trent. At present teaching at West Surrey College of Art and Design; and Richmond Adult College.

Visitors by appointment only.

Maker of ceramic musical instruments, vessels and sculpture, working in earthenware with painted slip surfaces, burnished and polished, plus a limited use of glaze. The direction of the work is the result of a fusion of interests in the natural world, music and American Indian artefacts.

Visits to Workshop by appointment only.

John Huggins
Courtyard Pottery
Groundwell Farm
Upper Stratton
Swindon, Wilts
*Swindon 721111
(STD code 0793)*

John Jelfs
'The Pottery'
Clapton Row
Bourton-on-the-Water
Gloucestershire
GL54 2DN
*Bourton-on-the-Water
20173
(STD code 0451)*

Produces a range of distinctive plant pots in bright firing terracotta. His robust frost resistant plant pots range from very small pots for window sills and sideboards to large tubs and urns for gardens and patios. Many of the pots are decorated with a distinctive sun and rain motif. His range also includes parsley pots, wall pots, drainage saucers and troughs.

Visitors are welcome to the showroom and workshop, but a telephone call first is advisable.

Trained at Cheltenham Art College and then with Russell Collins for one year. Set up present workshop in 1973 and at present producing domestic stoneware plus many one-offs, with wax resist and slip decoration. Large showroom within workshop.

Visitors welcome, but advisable to telephone if travelling long distances. Open most days.

ristopher Jenkins
ie Barn, Brook Lane
all Hill Road
ibcross,
dham
ancs OL3 5BQ

efers working in oxidised stoneware and at present produces a riety of decorated individual pieces. Trained as a painter at the ide School and as a potter at the Central School, London. nior lecturer in ceramics at Manchester Polytechnic.

Walter Keeler
Moorcroft Cottage
Penallt
Monmouth
Gwent NP5 4AH
Monmouth 3946
(STD code 0600)

Functional pottery of an individual nature in saltglazed stoneware.

Visitors by appointment only.

avid Lloyd Jones
ilford House
  Fulford
ork YO1 4PJ
ork 33331
TD code 0904)

akes a wide range of oil fired stoneware and porcelain.

owroom open daily 9.00-6.00 and visitors are welcome to see e workshop.

Colin Kellam
Lion Brewery
South Street
Totnes
Devon
Totnes 863158
(STD code 0803)

Domestic stoneware and large individual pieces. Standard range of four basic glazes decorated with brushwork. Designed his own large one chamber oil fired kiln. Trained at Loughborough College of Art 1959/1963. Worked with Marianne de Trey for four years where he built a wood fired kiln. Started present workshop 1969. Employs 3 full time people and one part-time. Takes students for a minimum 3 year stay.

Visitors welcome at showroom.

Danny Killick
School House
Mentmore
Leighton Buzzard
Beds
Cheddington 668 436
(STD code 0296)

Trained at Walthamstow School of Art and Harrow School of
Art. Established present workshop in 1970. Makes a range of
work using various bodies, mostly high fired, and a variety of
decorative techniques. Has exhibited at CPA, Bohun Gallery,
Crafts Council Touring Exhibition, various group exhibitions in
England and Europe. Recently teaching two days a week at
Harrow School of Art.

Peter Lane
The White House
Keswick Road
Cringleford
Norwich NR4 6UG
Norwich 55002
(STD code 0603)

Trained at Bath Academy of Art, Corsham. Works almost
exclusively in porcelain. Individual pieces, especially finely carved
porcelain bowls. Widely exhibited in Britain and overseas.
Represented in many private and public collections. Senior
Lecturer in Ceramics and Art Education at the University of East
Anglia, Norwich. Fellow of the Society of Designer-Craftsmen.
Works alone. Author of 'Studio Porcelain' (Pitman 1980) and
'Studio Ceramics' (Collins 1983)

Visitors by appointment only.

Ruth King
Fulford House
45 Fulford
York YO1 4PJ
York 33331
(STD code 0904)

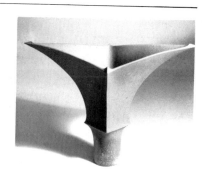

Individual handbuilt stoneware pots utilizing various techniques
of earthenware notably coiling and slabbing. Most items oxidised
stoneware fired in an electric kiln. Two or three glazes are
sprayed on for variation in both colour and surface quality with
glaze-on-glaze brush decoration on some pieces.

Visitors welcome by appointment.

David Leach
Lowerdown Pottery
Bovey Tracey
Devon
Bovey Tracey 833408
(STD code 0626)

Works with one or two assistants. Thrown stoneware and
porcelains of both domestic and individual character ranging in
price from 50p to £20 for domestic work and £3 to £100 for more
individual pieces. Started potting at 19 in 1930 with his father
Bernard Leach. Worked with him as student, manager and
partner until 1956 when started present workshop. Several one
man shows in England and USA. Work included in many
museums. Past chairman CPA. Gold medallist Istanbul 1967.
Lectures, designs kilns and researches into glazes.

Visitors welcome at showroom 9.00 — 6.00 weekdays and
9.00 — 1.00 Saturdays. Visitors to workshop by appointment
only.

net Leach
he Leach Pottery
Ives
rnwall
nzance 796398
TD code 0736)

Eileen Lewenstein
11 Western Esplanade
Portslade
Brighton
East Sussex BN4 1WE
Brighton 418705
(STD code 0273)

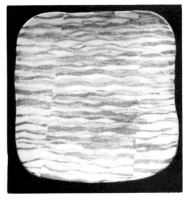

as held regular one potter exhibitions in England and Japan
d has participated in many group exhibitions. Work is included
the collections of Boymann's Museum, Rotterdam; Bristol
useum of Art; Stoke on Trent School of Art; London
epartment of Education; Newark Museum of Art, USA; Victoria
d Albert Museum, London; Cardiff Museum of Art; Derbyshire
epartment of Education; Bradford City Art Gallery; Bradford
useum Educational Services.

owroom is open to visitors and the workshop open to working
tters who should arrange such visits in advance.

Individual pots and objects in stoneware and porcelain.
Occasional architectural commisssions. Moved from London and
set up new studio in Hove, 1976. Work exhibited widely in this
country and abroad including Belgium 1981, Vallauris 1982, New
Zealand 1982,83, U.S.A. 1983. Represented in many public and
private collections Victoria and Albert Museum: Museum of
Decorative Arts, Prague: Tennessee Arts Commission U.S.A.:
Villeroy and Boch, Mettlach. Co-Editor *Ceramic Review*. Co-
Edited with Emmanuel Cooper 'New Ceramics' Studio Vista 1974.
Prices £10-£250.

Visitors welcome by appointment.

---

hn Leach
uchelney Pottery
uchelney
angport
merset
angport 250324
TD code 0458)

John Lomas
12 The Green
Jordans
nr Beaconsfield
Bucks HP9 2SU
Chalfont St Giles 4556
(STD code 02407)

omestic stoneware. Works with one assistant.

etail shop Mon — Fri 9.00 — 1.00, 2.00 — 6.00 Sat. 9.00 —
2.00. Wholesale enquiries welcome. Workshop by appointment
nly.

Thrown domestic and individual pieces in stoneware, reduction
fired. Self taught and works alone in small but well equipped
workshop.

Visitors welcome by appointment only.

Andrew McGarva
Wobage Farm
Upton Bishop
Ross-on-Wye
Herefordshire
HR9 7QP
Upton Bishop 233
(STD code 098 985)

Decorated tiles, large garden pots, domestic and decorative wares. Wood-fired and wood-fired saltglazed stoneware.

Showroom open at all reasonable times. Visitors to workshops please telephone first.

Jim Malone
c/o Cumbria College of Art
Brampton Road
Carlisle

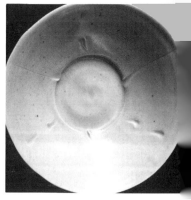

Currently teaching full time, and making a small amount of stoneware and porcelain.

Mal Magson
2 Mill Cottages
East Lutton
Malton
North Yorkshire
YO17 8TG
West Lutton 683
(STD code 094 43)
(Bowls unmarked)

Individual pieces of unglazed, handbuilt stoneware with agate decoration. Trained at Loughborough College of Art and Design 1969/72. Has been potting since 1973 and exhibited in the provinces, London and Hamburg.

No showroom. Visitors to tiny workshop by appointment only and in limited numbers.

John Maltby
Stoneshill Pottery
Stoneshill
Crediton
Devon
Crediton 2753
(STD code 036 32)

MALTBY

Individual pieces in oxidised and reduced stoneware, some with enamel decoration. Trained as sculptor. Studied pottery with Gordon Baldwin and David Leach. Started present pottery in 1965. Solo exhibitions in Britain and abroad. Gold Medal Faenza 1974. Visiting lecturer Bergen Kunsthandverksskole, West Surrey College of Art Farnham, Carlisle College of Art.

Visitors welcome but not on Sundays. Please telephone if making a special journey from a distance.

ctor Margrie
oke House
oke.
aminster
rset
8 3PD
aminster 862335
TD code 0308)

Leo Francis Matthews
Ivy House
Shawbury
Shropshire
Shawbury 759
(STD code 093 94)

dividual porcelain pieces. Trained at Hornsey College of Art
ow Middlesex Polytechnic). Three one-potter shows at the
itish Crafts Centre. Represented in various collections including
e Victoria and Albert Museum. Former Head of Ceramics,
arrow School of Art. Now Director, Crafts Council. Not potting
present time.

Produces sculptural ceramics, murals and some domestic studio
pottery, working in earthenware, reduced stoneware and some
porcelain. Exhibited in Britain and occasionally abroad. Studied
graphics at Manchester College of Art and ceramics at Stoke on
Trent College of Art.

Visitors by appointment only.

est Marshall
ring Lodge
undford Road
ethwold.
hetford
orfolk IP26 4RN
ethwold 728826
TD code 036 67)

Peter Meanley
6 Downshire Road
Bangor
Co Down
Bangor 66831
(STD code 0247)

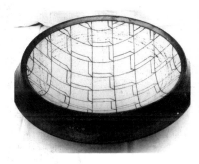

omestic and individual stoneware. Trained at Harrow School of
rt and teaching there. part-time, since 1977.

ew workshop under construction and due to be completed by
te 1983. No showroom.

Individual stoneware items incorporating a range of making
processes. I generally work in themes and alternate between
bowls, teapots and clocks. Function is not a primary consideration
and increasingly line and colour through slips and pattern are
augmenting longstanding interests with the movement and the
interchangeability of parts. I normally oxidise though recently
have lowered my optimum temperature from cone 9 to cone 6.
Course Leader Ceramics, Ulster Polytechnic. Occasional help
from wife.

Visitors welcome, though telephone appointment advisable.

William Mehornay
52 Worple Way
Richmond
Surrey
(01) 940 5051

Works in porcelain making a wide range of functional individual pieces — primarily bowls, dishes and flower vases — in a variety of glazes including yellows, blues, celadons and copper reds.

Visitors are welcome at the studio showroom. For opening times, please telephone.

David Miller
33 St. Andrew's Square
Surbiton
Surrey

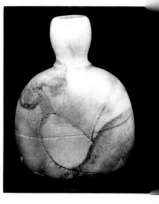

Mainly Raku and low temperature salt. Present pots are based on simple enclosed forms which are remodelled after throwing. Surface treatment obtained from copper saturated slip. Colours ranging from subtle browns and greens through to iridescent pinks and reds. Exhibitions in England, Germany and France.

No showroom; viewing by prior arrangement.

Eric James Mellon
5 Parkfield Avenue
Bognor Regis
Sussex PO21 3BW
Pagham 3221
(STD code 024 32)

Stoneware, individual pieces using wood ash glazes and brush drawn decoration. Born 1925. Studied Watford, Harrow and the Central School of Arts and Crafts, London. One-man exhibitions include: 1983 Folkestone Arts Centre. 1982 Katharine House Gallery, Marlborough. 1981 Westminster Gallery, Boston USA. 1978 David Paul Gallery, Chichester. 1974 Portsmouth Museum. 1971 Commonwealth Institute, London. 1969 Abbott Hall Art Gallery, Kendal. Group Exhibitions: 1982 International Symposium Cork, Ireland. 1979 & 77 British Crafts Centre. 1973 British Potters' Works, Japan. 1972 International Ceramics, Victoria and Albert Museum. Work in private and public collections.

Clients by appointment only.

David Morris
Biergate Cottage
Main Road
Grainthorpe
Louth
Lincolnshire
LN11 7HX
Marshchapel 260
(STD code 0472 86)

Usually works alone producing a full range of standard domestic ware, but with a proportion of individual pieces. Oxidised stoneware glazed white with blue floral, brushed and resist decoration sold mainly through craft shops and galleries. Commemorative lettered plates. Mainly wholesale with prices from £1 to about £50.

Visitors and retail customers welcome any reasonable time, but it is advisable to telephone first.

ryan Newman
ne Pottery
ller
angport
merset
A10 0QN
angport 250 244
TD code 0458)

orks in partnership with wife and one assistant. Utilitarian ware
d ceramic sculpture, reduced stoneware. Trained at
amberwell School of Arts and Crafts. Exhibited widely in this
untry and abroad. Prices: Domestic ware £1 — £25, Sculpture
8 — £60.

isitors welcome at showroom dawn to dusk.

**Magdalene
A.N.Odundo**
Talisman
Send Marsh Road
Ripley
Surrey GU23 6JN
Guildford 224345
(STD code 0483)

Odundo '83

Hand built burnished oxidised and reduced ceramics.

Workshop. Visitors welcome but please telephone before arrival.

ileen Nisbet
5 Millman Street
olborn
ondon WC1N 3EP
1) 242 7362

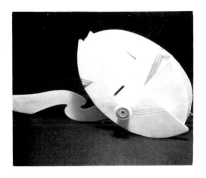

rained at Hornsey School of Art and Central School of Art and
Design, London. Has taken part in many exhibitions in London,
witzerland, Germany, Boston and New York, USA. At present
orking in porcelain, and teaching at Central School of Art and
Design, London.

Warwick Parker
The Dairy House
Maiden Newton
Dorchester
Dorset
Maiden Newton 20414
(STD code 0300)

Wide range of individual and domestic stoneware. Trained at
Poole Pottery as trainee thrower, then attended Poole School of
Art. Finally worked with David Leach for 3½ years. Started
present pottery in 1967.

Visitors welcome at showroom. 9.00 — 6.00 weekdays, 9.00 —
1.00 Saturdays. Please telephone if making special journey.
Wholesale enquiries welcome. Commissions undertaken.

Colin Pearson
3 Mountford Terrace
Barnsbury Square
Islington
London N1 1JJ
(01) 607 1965
Studio and Showroom
15-17 Cloudsley Road
London N1

Makes individual pieces in porcelain and stoneware. Trained in painting at Goldsmith's College. Worked under Ray Finch and David Leach. Started present pottery in 1961. Exhibits widely in UK and abroad. 1975 winner of 33rd Premio Faenza. Part-time teaching at Camberwell and Medway College of Design.

Visitors welcome by appointment. 5 minutes Angel underground. Easy parking.

Ian Pirie
8 St. Michael's Road
Newtonhill
Stonehaven
Kincardineshire
Stonehaven 30908
(STD code 0569)

Lecturer in Ceramics, Gray's School of Art, Aberdeen. Work mainly high-fired porcelain, both oxidised and reduced, with airbrushed and hand-drawn decoration.

Visitors by appointment.

Peter Phillips
Ivy Cottage
Taylors Lane
Trottiscliffe
Kent
Fairseat 822901
(STD code 0732)

Peter Phillips works with his wife Julie in the village of Trottiscliffe, Kent. He handbuilds boxes of various sizes in the form of boats, and Julie makes decorative boxes. These are reduced stoneware and porcelain using various slip glazes. These are sold through galleries in the U.K. and on the Continent. *Peter also does quite a lot of throwing, making bread crocks, casseroles, bowls and jugs, although these are normally for 'local consumption'. There is an increasing interest in Belgium and France. Peter and Julie have now a studio in France. (Dordogne) with an oil-fired kiln. They work there for several weeks a year producing a similar range of work but using local materials. Peter is in charge of the pottery course at Medway College of Design.*

Katharine Pleydell-Bouverie
Kilmington Manor
Near Warminster
Wiltshire
BA12 6RD
Maiden Bradley 259
(STD code 098 53)

Stoneware mainly pots and bowls for flowers. Prices roughly 50p to £15. Trained at Central School of Art and Leach Pottery. St. Ives. Work in various collections including Victoria and Albert Museum, British Museum and Boymans. Works alone and has no showroom, but visitors are normally welcome to the workshop by appointment.

hn Pollex
rbican Craft
orkshops
White Lane
rbican
ymouth PL1 2LP
ymouth 662338
TD code 0752)

ained at Harrow School of Art 1968-1970. Assistant to Bryan
ewman and Colin Pearson. Present workshop established 1971.
orks with one assistant producing domestic slipware and
dividual pieces. Teaches part-time at Medway College of Design
d Plymouth School of Art. Author of 'Slipware' (Pitman) 1979.
ember Devon Guild of Craftsmen.

sitors welcome to showroom 9am — 5.30pm Monday-Saturday.

Vicki Read
Claycutters
Studio Pottery
Sheep Street (A413)
Winslow
Buckingham
Bucks
Winslow 2663
(STD code 029671)

Works with her husband Bill Read, in high fired reduction
stoneware, fired in a natural gas kiln. Makes very large pieces,
bowls and other forms, mainly to commission. Also a range of
domestic ware. Has exhibited widely.

Open day-time and weekends.

eorge Rainer
Nugent Hill
istol
66 5TD
ristol 48403
TD code 0272)

akes one-off pieces in coloured clays, decorating mainly by
lay.

Stanislas Reychan
MBE
Garden Studio
3 Acacia Road
London NW8 6AB
(01) 722 1285

Modelled figures and ornaments. Born 1897. Trained at St.
Martin's School of Art and Central School of Arts and Crafts
under Dora Billington. Has exhibited at the R.A. Design Centre
and has had many one-man shows. Paris Salon Bronze Medal
1958, Silver Medal 1960.

Mary A. Rich
Penwerris Pottery
Cowlands Creek
Old Kea
nr Truro
Cornwall TR3 6AT
Truro 76926
(STD code 0872)

Stoneware, porcelain and bone china, all once fired in an oil-fired kiln. Slip glazes applied to most pots with the addition of a light saltglaze. Many of the porcelain pots are decorated with on glaze lustre. Works alone therefore advisable to telephone before visiting the workshop.

David Roberts
Cressfield House
44 Upperthong Lane
Holmfirth
Huddersfield
West Yorkshire
HD7 1BQ
Huddersfield 685110
(STD code 0484)

At present work consists solely of handbuilt Raku fired vessels. The work shows a concern with simplicity of form and a fascination with and control over surface incident arising from the firing processes. Gentle curves and tensions within the form are sometimes played against hard edge, geometric decoration. These simple marks and lines also indicate the main dynamics within the form and contrast with the random quality of the glazed surface. Some recent work is subjected to several slip and glaze firings before the final Raku process.

No showroom but visitors are welcome to workshop by appointment.

Christine-Ann Richards
14a Percy Circus
London WC1X 9ES
(01) 833 1898

CAR

I have always been excited by oriental ceramics and since visiting China in 1978 that interest has become specifically Chinese. The quality of glazes — especially the crackle or Kuan has been a constant source of inspiration and it is these qualities which I have sought to bring to my work. Works with porcelain fired to approximately 1280°C.

Visitors to studio by appointment only. Work for sale.

James W. Robison
Robison Ceramics
3 Booth House Lane
Holmfirth
Huddersfield HD7 1QA
Huddersfield 68 5270
(STD code 0484)

Works in stoneware and Raku. Studied sculpture and ceramics in the U.S.A., Senior Lecturer in ceramics/sculpture at Bretton Hall College. Creates individual pieces using slabware techniques. Eroded earth formations, standing stones, fossils, and Celtic designs have inspired recent work. Often works on a large scale. Commissions undertaken.

Visitors welcome during gallery hours 2-5pm Saturday and Sunday, and by appointment.

Mary Rogers
Brook Farm House
Nanpantan Road
Loughborough
Leicestershire
LE11 3YE
Loughborough 239205
(STD code 0509)

Ray Silverman
35 Dunster Crescent
Hornchurch
Essex
Hornchurch 58864
(STD code 040 24)

Has been making handbuilt individual ceramics since 1960, working in porcelain and stoneware. Her book 'On pottery and stoneware-A Hand-Builder's Approach' was published in Britain, Germany and USA 1979 (new edition 1983) and her methods of making pinch and coil-built ceramics were described in her article *Ceramic Review* No. 38. They were also demonstrated by her in 'The Craft of the Potter' on BBC TV. Her work widely exhibited in Britain and abroad, and work is in the collections of The Metropolitan Museum, New York; The Museum of Modern Art, New York; The Victoria and Albert Museum, London; Fitzwilliam Museum, Cambridge, and museums in Germany, Australia, New Zealand and Norway.

Works alone and has no private showroom.

Trained at Camberwell School of Art and Crafts. Exhibited in U.K. and abroad. Worked for several years as designer for a large overseas company, where he is still retained as a consultant. Lecturer in Ceramics and Design at West Ham College. Produces domestic and individual pieces, stoneware and procelain.

David Scott
31 Athelstane Grove
Bow
London E3 5JG
(01) 981 6781

D.S.

M.C. Skipwith
Lotus Pottery
Stoke Gabriel
Totnes
South Devon
TQ9 6SL
Stoke Gabriel 303
(STD code 080 428)

The work at present alternates between one-off non functional pieces and domestic pottery, which consists mainly of a small range of teapots, storage jars, jugs etc., and a few large pedestal jardinieres. I use a red earthenware body, bisque-fired to 1150°C and glazed to 1050°C. The glaze is usually used only to seal the inside surfaces, the exteriors of the pots are largely unglazed, relying on small distortions of form, and surface quality for decoration. The non-functional pieces are based notionally on the container and are slab-built and incorporate pressmoulding and some mixed media.

No showroom. Visitors by appointment only.

Works with Elizabeth Skipwith in part of a vast old stonebuilt farm building converted to workshop and showroom. Wide range of tableware and individual pieces in earthenware, stoneware and porcelain.

Visitors welcome to showroom and West Country Craft Gallery. Monday to Friday 9am — 1pm, 2pm — 6pm Saturday 10am — 1pm.

Mildred Slatter
The White Cottage
Framewood Road
Stoke Poges
Bucks SL2 4QR
Fulmer 3249
(STD code 028 16)

Stoneware and porcelain, domestic and sculptural work. Trained at Reading Universtiy and Central School. Has exhibited at High Wycombe, London, Oxford, Chalfont St. Giles, Southampton and Bath. Fellow of The Society of Designer Craftsmen.

Visitors welcome to showroom and workshop at any time but please telephone beforehand.

Peter Smith
Bojewyan Pottery
Higher Bojewyan
Pendeen
Penzance
Cornwall TR19 7TR
Penzance 788820
(STD code 0736)

Earthenware pottery often slip decorated and flame flashed, fired in a large single chamber coal burning kiln. Current interests are the application of innovations in technique to functional pottery and non-functional clay forms.

Visitors are welcome at any reasonable time.

Frank Smith
Old Winders House
Peasmarsh
Nr Rye
Sussex
Peasmarch 284
(STD code 079 721)

Spent year with Colin Pearson making pots. Works alone producing raw glazed domestic stoneware and porcelain using catenary arch trolley hearth oil fired kiln. House easily found on A268 road 4 miles from Rye.

Visitors welcome at any reasonable time.

John Solly
36 London Road
Maidstone
Kent ME16 8QL
Maidstone 54623
(STD code 0622)

Established the pottery in 1953, in buildings which had been built originally as a basket works in about 1820. Started making pots at Maidstone School of Art in 1945, under the guidance of Percy Brown, and later, Gwylym Thomas. Spent very short working periods with Wally Cole at Rye, and Ray Finch at Winchcombe. Runs courses each year at the pottery at Easter, and mid-June to September. 1984 will be the Silver Jubilee year. Was the founder chairman of the now very active Kent Potters Association. Sells direct from the pottery, and at the CPA and St. James's Gallery, Bath. Domestic repetition and individual pots in earthenware and slipware at 1120°C and mid temperature at 1160/1180°C. Red and Buff clays with added local sand.

Gary Standige
500 Station Road
Aylesford
Kent
Maidstone 70730
(STD code 0622)

Currently making thrown forms in high-fired stoneware and porcelain. Lecturer in ceramics at West Surrey College of Art and Design.

Visitors welcome by appointment.

Peter Starkey
12 Wordsworth Avenue
Roath
Cardiff
Cardiff 498362
(STD code 0222)

Saltglazed stoneware domestic and individual pieces. Lecturer in Ceramics at Cardiff College of Art.

Visitors by appointment.

Ann Stannard
Ty-Newydd
Off Mill Road
Holyhead
Gwynedd
Holyhead 50275
(STD code 0407)

Working with Karen Karnes at Ty-Newydd January to April and in Morgan, Vermont, U.S.A. May to December. One-of-a-kind pieces stoneware. Oil fired.

Peter Stoodley
15 Gordon Road
Boscombe
Bournemouth
BH1 4DW
Bournemouth 36766
(STD code 0202)

Mostly garden pots. Hand built vitreous slip decorated, electric fired stoneware. Maximum size 17″ x 18″ £35-£90. Started potting at Camberwell School of Art in 1947.

Visitors welcome by appointment.

Warren & Debora Storch
Lawers Farm Pottery
Comrie
Perthshire
Comrie 70207
(STD code 0764)

Helen Swain
8 Fyfield Road
Waltham Forest
London E17 3RG
(01) 520 4043

Individual and functional stoneware and porcelain. Studied painting, pottery with Helen Pincombe, and terracotta at Willesden then Hornsey College of Art. Short time with Harry and May Davis, then three very happy years with Agnete Hoy at Royal Doulton, Lambeth decorating saltglaze stoneware. Has taught part-time since 1952, from 1963 at Goldsmith's College, London. Solus exhibition at CPA 1961 and eleven group exhibitions since.

This is a one woman pottery in a family home, so visitors by appointment only, and sorry no students possible at present.

Harry Horlock Stringer
Taggs Yard
School of Ceramics
11½ Woodlands Rd
Barnes
London SW13 0JZ
(01) 876 5750

Geoffrey Swindell
35 Murch Road
Dinas Powis
Cardiff CF6 4RD
Cardiff 512746
(STD code 0222)

At present working in oxidised stoneware producing articles for personal use. Iron slip decorating techniques used with a limited number of glazes. Small amount of individual work is also made in porcelain and stoneware. Trained originally as a painter/silversmith. Self taught as a potter. Work exhibited Tokyo, Paris, Prague, Glasgow, London and the provinces. For the benefit of potters and students of pottery from all parts of the world an international summer school is held in Tagg's Yard every July/August.

Visitors by appointment only.

Works in porcelain making individual, small scale, wheel made pots. Studied Stoke on Trent and Royal College of Art 1960-1970. Exhibited widely in Britain and abroad, represented in many museum and private collections. Fellow of Society of Designer Craftsmen, member of International Academy of Ceramics. Lecturer in ceramics at South Glamorgan Institute of Higher Education (Cardiff).

Visitors by appointment only.

anice Tchalenko
0 Therapia Road
London SE22
(01) 693 1624

Trained at Harrow School of Art. Works alone, making domestic reduced stoneware. Uses coloured slip trailed and painted glazes for decoration. Teaches part-time at Camberwell School of Art and Crafts and Royal College of Art.

Visitors by appointment only.

Vera Tollow
5 Woodcote Mews
Wallington
Surrey
(01) 647 9898

Works in reduced stoneware and porcelain, with ash glazes, fired in gas kiln. Makes a wide range of functional pots as well as one-off large pieces for commissions and exhibitions. Studio too small to accommodate students.

Visitors by appointment only.

Owen Thorpe
Churchstoke Pottery
Old School
Churchstoke
Powys SY15 6AG
Churchstoke 511
(STD code 058 85)

The workshop is housed in an old chapel in remote unspoilt West Shropshire. Makes range of oxidised stoneware including coffee sets, teapots, tea sets, mugs, jugs, bowls, casseroles, stock pots, egg bakers, goblets, carafes etc. An increasing proportion of production now given over to individual pots. Glazes used are mainly felspathic and extensive use made of local clay as slip. Works at the moment with one assistant. It is hoped that accommodation will be available in due course for those who wish to combine pottery with a country holiday.

Visitors to workshop and showroom are welcome. Telephone beforehand to avoid disappointment.

Marianne de Trey
Shinners Bridge
Pottery
Dartington
Totnes, Devon
TQ9 6JB
Totnes 862046
(STD code 0803)

Mostly hand thrown porcelain; reduction fired in propane kiln.

Visitors preferably by appointment.

17

Angela Verdon
Gladstone Pottery
Museum
Uttoxeter Road
Longton
Stoke-on-Trent
Staffs
Stoke-on-Trent 319232
(STD code 0782)

At present I am working exclusively in bone china. The one-off pieces are finely cast with incised and pierced surfaces which utilise and enhance the translucency of the medium. Due to the extreme thinness the cast pieces are first fired to 1120°C. More recently I have incorporated colour which is applied by trailing body stains onto the surface of the mould and then cast in the usual manner. Once the surface decoration is applied the pieces are fired to 1220°C with a two hour soak and finally burnished to achieve a semi-matt sheen.

"I have a showroom and welcome visitors by appointment only".

Sarah Walton
'Keepers'
Selmeston
Nr. Polegate
East Sussex
BN26 6UH
Ripe 517 and 284
(STD code 032 183)

Trained first as a painter, but switched to studio pottery in 1972, training at Harrow. Her pots are either thrown or handbuilt, in stoneware or porcelain, and all are saltglazed. Accepts orders, bearing in mind that due to the nature of the technique no pot is ever exactly like another. Raw fires to 1300°C and uses an oil fired down-draught. Works alone.

Visitors welcome to showroom especially those who telephone beforehand.

Alan Wallwork
Ceramics
Burton Street
Marnhull
Dorset
Marnhull 820460
(STD code 0258)

Decorative stoneware, terracotta and tiles. Tries to keep a varied reserve of work to supply callers and wholesale customers 'off the shelf' as does not like making pottery to order. Is now limiting all production to allow more experiment and time off.

John Ward
Fachongle Uchaf
Cilgwyn
Newport
Dyfed SA42 0GR
Newport 820 706
(STD code 0239)

All of my work is handbuilt by pinching out a base then adding strips of clay. I use an electric kiln, each pot being biscuit fired then glaze fired to 1250°C. Glazes are applied by a combination of pouring and spraying, sometimes with oxides underneath rubbed into texture or applied in banded designs. I am interested in simple hollow forms, especially bowls, function being secondary to form. The insides and outsides are equally important and it is the interplay between these and the feeling of hollowness which I explore.

Visitors by appointment.

Robin Welch

Robin Welch Pottery
Stradbroke
Diss
Norfolk
Stradbroke 416
(STD code 037 984)

Mary White

Zimmerplatzweg 6
6551 Wonsheim,
West Germany
Germany 06703 2922

The pottery is a mile out of Stradbroke on the B1118, Wilby Road, two hours from London. A range of domestic stoneware is produced using the jigger and jolley technique. Individual pots and sculpture are also made. A basic feldspar glaze with wood ash gives rich earthy colours fired in a 100 cu. ft. trolly hearth kiln to 1300°C in a reduced atmosphere. Domestic ware has been accepted by the Council of Industrial Design and exhibited in the Design Centre regularly. Trained at Nuneaton and Penzance School of Art, worked part-time at the Leach Pottery, St. Ives, and at Central School of Art and Design, London. Spent three years working in Australia. Exhibited in many countries and pots in many museums and galleries.

Visitors welcome 10.00 — 6.00
Monday to Saturday.

Mainly individual porcelain pieces. Thrown and handbuilt forms, ranging from her well-known 'Flanged Bowls' to experimental ceramic sculptures. Work represented in many museums and private collections in Great Britain, U.S.A. and Germany. Moved to Germany in 1980, shortly after teaching at the International Atlantic College. In 1982 was awarded the Staatspreis (Federal Prize) for Rheinland-Phalz, West Germany.

Visitors welcome by appointment.

Tony Weston

Little Cokenach
Nuthampstead
Nr. Royston
Herts
Barkway 464
(STD code 076 384)

Geoffrey Whiting

St. Augustine's Pottery
2 Monastery Street
Canterbury
Kent CT1 1NJ
Canterbury 57064
(STD code 0227)

A wide range of once fired domestic stoneware. Oil fired kiln, reduction glazes.

Visitors welcome but please telephone first.

Basic production of domestic stoneware, supplemented by more individual work in stoneware and hard porcelain.

Visitors by appointment.

Caroline Whyman
15 Swan Yard
Highbury Station Road
London N1 1SD
(01) 226 9403

Studied ceramics at Camberwell School of Art. Makes individual thrown porcelain; mostly bowls, vases, boxes and covered jars often with carved and trailed decoration in an electric kiln, as well as some larger pieces in stoneware, and occasionally Raku. The workshop, which was originally a stable in an industrial mews in Islington, is shared with one other potter working independently.

Visitors are welcome at the workshop, but please telephone first for suitable times and directions to Swan Yard.

Mollie Winterburn
Tancnwch
Ystradmeurig
Dyfed
Pontrhydfendigaid 275
(STD code 097 45)

Potting, painting and printmaking in glorious mid-Wales. Still making bottles and abstract sculptural pieces — everything one-off, mainly stoneware. Is the author of books on handbuilding with clay in Britain and U.S.A.

David Winkley
Vellow Pottery
Lower Vellow
Williton
Taunton
Somerset
Stogumber 458
(STD code 098 46)

Works with his assistant, Tim Jay, making a very wide range of thrown, reduction fired stoneware for domestic use together with individual pieces in both stoneware and porcelain. Author of 'Pottery' (Pelham Books 1974) a practical guide to pottery making methods, kiln design and building, glazing and kiln firing.

Retail showroom on premises. Visitors welcome to both workshop and showroom between 8.30 a.m. and 6 p.m. Monday to Saturday.

Nigel Wood
Meon Pottery
Lippen Hill
Church Lane
West Meon
Petersfield
Hampshire
West Meon 434
(STD code 073 086)

MEON

A potter since 1966. Trained at traditional potteries followed by a three-year course at West Surrey College of Art and Design, and six months with stoneware potter Peter Arnold. Established Meon Pottery in partnership in 1973 and made terracotta garden pots, stoneware and porcelain, using a large two-chambered oil-fired kiln. Very interested in Far Eastern glazes and porcelains ('Oriental Glazes' Pitman 1978). Still working at West Meon when possible, but presently also Research Lecturer in Art History and Lecturer in ceramic theory at West Surrey College of Art and Design.

Visitors welcome but telephone call essential.

osemary D. Wren
he Oxshott Pottery
ill Cottage
ustleigh
ewton Abbot
evon
ustleigh 231
TD code 064 77)

osemary Wren works in partnership with Peter Crotty *q.v.*
lakes simple hollow handbuilt animal and bird forms. Colours
toneware glazes and oxides) — normally filled in by Peter Crotty
ho also fires the kiln. The Pottery founded at Oxshott, Surrey in
)20 by her parents Denise and Henry Wren. She helped set up
e CPA in 1956, and was a council member until 1972
Chairman 1958—65). Work is in many collections and has
chibited widely.

me work usually available retail. Visitors welcome but please
lephone. Turn west at the signpost 3 miles north of Bovey
racey on the A382.

Takeshi Yasuda
16 Station Road
South Molton
Devon
South Molton 2829
(STD code 076 95)

Trained and worked in Mashiko, Japan for ten years with four-
chambered climbing kiln. In 1973 came to England with Sandy
Brown to set up workshop. Works mainly on functional
stoneware; glazed and unglazed, gas and wood-fired and some
salt ware. Taught extensively in England, Wales, Norway and
Denmark; and demonstrated in various places including Germany
and Sweden. Teaches part-time at West Surrey College of Art and
Design.

Showroom open all year round. Monday — Saturday 10 a.m. to 5
p.m.. Potters and students are welcome to the workshop.

Iuriel Wright
.ldringham Craft
1arket
ir Leiston
uffolk IP16 4PY
.eiston 830397
iTD code 0728)

xidised stoneware. Garden pots and thrown and handbuilt
irms in raku. Trained at Manchester College of Art. Been
otting for 25 years.

'isitors welcome at showroom all year round.
:0 a.m. — 5.30 p.m. daily

'losed Sundays.

Poh Chap Yeap
Stable House
Pitch Hill
Ewhurst
Surrey SY6 7NN
Cranleigh 277494
(STD code 0483)

Wheel thrown porcelain and stoneware bowls, dishes, teapots,
bottles etc. in the Chinese tradition. Glazes are usual traditional
like celadons, crackled, white, copper reds, uranium yellows, dark
browns (tenmoku) etc. Trained at Hammersmith College of Art
and Building and the Royal College of Art. Member British
Crafts Centre, International Academy of Ceramics, elected
member of Society of Designer-Craftsmen. Work in Ashmolean
Museum, Hetjens Museum, Dusseldorf. Many one-man
exhibitions since 1973 in Britain and overseas.

Visitors by appointment.

Andrew and Joanna Young
Common Farm
Sustead Road
Lower Gresham
Norfolk NR11 8RE
Matlaske 548
(STD code 026 377)

A & J YOUNG

Trained at West Surrey College of Art and Design, Farnham. Set up workshop in 1975, moved to Gresham in 1981. At present firing 90 cu. ft. oil kiln, mainly producing wide range of raw glazed domestic stoneware. Occasional exhibitions.

No showroom. Visitors please telephone.

Monica Young
Old Butcher's Yard
Reeth
nr Richmond
North Yorkshire
Reeth 487
(STD code 074 884)

Makes large coiled pots, maximum size 55 × 36 inches. The pots are unglazed, but fired to 1300°C in a reducing atmosphere, acquire a deep honey colour. The pots are frost-proof.

Visitors by appointment please.

So You Want to be a Potter

Pottery Training in the United Kingdom

The opportunities for learning pottery vary from full time study at art school to teaching yourself from books. In this section all the possibilities are detailed under different headings.

Workshop Training

Because of the very diverse nature of craft pottery no formal apprenticeship scheme exists for training prospective potters. The kind of work undertaken by trainees, and the amount and quality of the teaching they receive in the workshop, will depend largely on the skill and outlook of the potter they work for.

Joining a workshop is not easy. The number of potters employing assistants is small, demand for places exceeds supply, and competition is, therefore, fierce. Success in finding a potter to work with will require a high level of commitment, strong perseverence and almost certainly some measure of luck.

You can try to join a pottery direct as a trainee assistant or for a period of workshop practice following an art school ceramics course. One with a strong bias towards craft pottery would be an advantage.

The work of some potters is so individual that it precludes additional help. Those who do employ assistants often spend much of their time making repetition ware decorative or functional. Students leaving art schools for workshops may find the change constricting. Much of the learning will inevitably be done by making pots designed intially by the teacher and the opportunities for personal expression are likely to be limited.

There are no standard rates of pay for trainees and renumeration will be set by potters according to their means and in relation to the real productive help that an assistant can give. It is the experience of many potters that students often overestimate their ability to make pots quickly and of a saleable quality. The Crafts Council offer a variety of Training Grant Schemes. Some are intended for established craftworkers and these are a great help in supplementing the wages of trainees. But this scheme is not automatically available to every potter with assistants and it must be assumed that rates of pay for trainees will be less — and in some cases considerably less — than those in industry or teaching.

The names and addresses of full members of the Craftsmen Potters Association are listed in this book. Many other potters are included in the 'Visitors Guide to Country Workshops' published by the Council for Small Industries in Rural Areas (CoSira) and in 'Craftsmen of Quality' published by the Crafts Council. Potters are also listed in Yellow Pages. One pottery training establishment, set up with the support of the Crafts Council, is the Dartington Pottery Training Workshop. This produces a range of domestic stoneware pottery and provides practical training for art college students and for apprentices wishing to make a career of craft pottery. Further details about this scheme can be obtained from the Workshop, Shinner's Bridge, Dartington, Totnes, Devon.

corner of the Dartington Pottery Training Workshop.

Application to Workshops

Before applying to workshops see the work of as many potters as you can so that you are clear about the kind of pots you want to make. If, for example, your main interest is ceramic sculpture you are likely to be happier working with a potter whose prime interest this is than one preoccupied with domestic ware. This obvious fact is often ignored and too few applicants apply to potters with whose work they are familiar and sympathetic.

Just writing a letter which says, in essence, 'I am interested in pottery. Do you have a job?' is unlikely to gain a positive response. Potters get many such letters from applicants who appear to post a dozen or so at a time to widely differing potters in the hope that something will turn up. It rarely does.

The better, and probably only, way is to go and see the potters of your choice in their workshops. This requires a lot of effort, it's time-consuming and demands perseverence mentioned earlier. But in seeking a workshop place you are, in effect, asking potters to make a commitment to you in time, energy and money. Potters have livings to earn and they must be as sure as they can that you are really serious about working with them to mutual advantage. In short they have to be convinced that there is something in it for them as well as you.

Before you visit telephone or write to see that it is convenient. Take with you any examples or photographs of pots you have made. Without some evidence it is very difficult for potters to judge an applicant's ability or potential.

Working successfully and harmoniously a a member of a small team, or in conjunction with an individual potter, is as much a question of good personal relationships as the teaching and acquisition of skills. In the search for workshop places, therefore, it is difficult to overestimate the value of personal contact. This works both ways: it enables potters to judge at first hand an applicant's response to the work they do and, equally important, it gives applicant's the opportunity to see what facilities are available and to say what they can offer the workshop. Trainees have much to give in enthusiasm for and commitment to working with clay, and in ready willingness to share all the many and sometimes tedious jobs that every workshop has to undertake to produce finished pots.

Useful Addresses

Craftsmen Potters Association
William Blake House
Marshall Street
London W1V 1FD

Council of Small Industries in Rural Areas (CoSIRA)
41 Castle Street
Salisbury
Wilts SP1 3TB

Welsh Arts Council
Museum Place
Cardiff

Crafts Council
12 Waterloo Place
London SW1 4AU

British Crafts Centre
43 Earlham Street
London WC2H 9LD

Scottish Arts Council
19 Charlotte Square
Edinburgh

Regional Arts Associations

Eastern Arts Association
8/9 Bridge Street
Cambridge

South East Arts Association
58 London Road
Southborough
Tunbridge Wells, Kent.

East Midland Arts Association
1 Frederick Street
Loughborough
Leicestershire

Greater London Arts Association
25 Tavistock Place
London WC1

Lincolnshire and Humberside Arts Association
Beaumont Lodge
Beaumont Fee
Lincoln

Merseyside Arts Association
Bluecoat Chambers
School Lane
Liverpool

Northern Arts Association
31 Newbridge Street
Newcastle-upon-Tyne

North West Arts Association
52 King Street
Manchester M2 4LY

Southern Arts Association
19 Southgate
Winchester

South West Arts Association
23 Southern Hay East
Exeter

West Midlands Arts Association
City Arcade
Birmingham B2 4TX

Yorkshire Arts Association
Glyde House
Glydegate
Bradford 5

North Wales Arts Association
Victoria Street
Cwmbran
Gwent NP4 3JP

West Wales Arts Association
Dark Gate, Red Street
Carmarthen, Dyfed

Part-time Tuition

Part-time courses
Part-time courses are generally classed as 'Non-vocational' though some are able, over a period of time, to provide a fairly thorough training in studio pottery techniques. Many Art Colleges, Technical Colleges and Colleges of Adult and Further Education (including some of the ones listed later) offer such courses, some giving their own certificate of proficiency. As the intake is irregular and the age and standard of students variable it is usual for each student to follow his/her own course of indefinite duration. Particulars of these and evening institutes in your area can be obtained from the local Adult Education Centre or from the Chief Education Officer of your Education Authority.

Evening and part-time classes
Most Local Education Authorities provide classes of this kind for beginners and also for the more advanced student. Classes last approximately 2 hours. Fees are relatively low. Materials are provided and finished work can be purchased at minimal cost. Personal tools are not usually provided. Instructors vary in skill and teaching ability and it is worth asking other students how they have fared. Full information on available classes can be obtained from your local Public Library or Education Office. In London the booklet 'Floodlight' lists all currently available classes and can be obtained through most newsagents and bookshops. New sessions start in September each year. It is worth remembering that pottery classes are usually the most popular so book early. However, some vacant places will occur during the year which can be taken up by new students.

Short courses
Art Colleges do not generally offer 'crash' courses; however a number of short (usually summer) courses are offered by public and private bodies and by individual potters. Particulars of these should be sought in the national educational or art press or in periodicals such as *'Ceramic Review'*, *'Pottery Quarterly'* and *'Crafts'*. Some potters run summer courses which may or may not be residential. Such courses are not cheap, but give excellent value for money. Equipment is good and the prospectus lists the aims of the course and the timetable. It may be worthwhile shopping around for the course that suits you best. Some of the well known potters' merchants run seminars for the amateur and professional potter. The National Institute of Adult Education publishes a booklet 'Residential Short Courses' twice a year in March and September. It can be obtained for 90p from National Institute of Adult Education, 19b De Montford Street, Leicester LE1 7GE.

Regular Courses

Harrogate College of Arts and Adult Studies
Victoria Avenue
Harrogate HG1 1EL

Iron Bridge Art Centre
3 Lower North Street
Exeter
Devon EX4 3ET

Kingsbury Pottery
Boyn Hill Road
Maidenhead
Berkshire

Mary McGregor
Roxburgh
Kelso
Scotland

Ridge Pottery
Queen Camel
Yeovil
Somerset

John Solly
36 London Road
Maidstone
Kent ME16 8QL

Taggs Yard School of Ceramics
11½ Woodlands Road
Barnes
London SW13 0JZ
(special courses for overseas groups)

White House Studio
Somersham
Ipswich
Suffolk

White Roding Pottery
Bretts Farm
White Roding
Dunmow, Essex

Wolfscastle Pottery
Wolfscastle
Nr. Haverfordwest
Dyfed

Wood End Pottery
Near Cuckney
Mansfield, Notts
(also courses for Norwegian speaking students)

Woodhampton House Pottery
Little Hereford
Ludlow
Salop

Occasional Courses

Adult Education Centre
Stychens Lane
Bletchingly
Nr. Redhill, Surrey

College of Craft Education
c/o Peter Dawson
52 Locarno Avenue
Gillingham, Kent ME8 6ES
(Courses held at Leeds Polytechnic and
West Dean College, Chichester)

Dove Workshops
Butleigh
Nr. Glastonbury
Somerset

Ginge Brook Pottery
East Hendred
Oxon.

Lyth Ceramic Workshop
Lyth
Caithness

St. Martin's College
Lancaster LA1 3JD

Sir John Cass School of Art
Whitechapel High Street
London E1

West Dean College
West Dean
Chichester
Sussex

Seminars

Clayglaze
1 High Street
Rickmansworth
Herts

Wharf Pottery
Godalming
Surrey

Full-time courses in art colleges and polytechnics

Graduate level courses BA (Hons)

These three or four year Courses preceded by a one or two year Foundation Course aim for the development of the individual rather than his/her training for a specific employment situation. Entry is highly competitive and educational requirements stringent (usually 5 GCE 'O' level passes, although some colleges demand one or two 'A' level passes). Pottery (Ceramics) is usually contained in three dimensional design 'area' and courses include compulsory work in other media and a proportion of Art History and Complementary Studies. In the Colleges offering Ceramics as a 'chief study' the emphasis varies widely between the poles of the craft, fine-art and industrial design pottery, though most make opportunities for all these in some degree. Intending students should study prospectuses or visit courses before making applications.

For residents in the UK grants for these courses are mandatory, once a place has been secured, but are subject to Means Test and other certain conditions. Overseas students may have to pay full fees and satisfy interviewing boards that they are financially viable.

Vocational courses

These courses differ from the above in these respects:

The entry requirements are usually less stringent.

The courses are geared more towards professional training for subsequent employment as technician, craftworker, designer/craftworker or designer.

Grants are at the discretion of the LEAs.

Courses vary from 2 – 4 years.

Courses, which usually lead to a local, regional or professional Diploma or Licentiateship include some ancillary studies in drawing, design and other craft techniques.

No official 'sandwich' courses for studio potters exist at present but some Colleges make informal arrangements for students to work in potters' workshops during the course or in vacations.

TOPS (Training Opportunities Scheme) intensive courses for potters have now been set up in some areas.

Colles offering full-time courses in ceramics

College	Course, Entry requirements and Qualifications

Amersham College of Further Education and Art
Stanley Hill
Amersham
Bucks HP7 9HN
Tel: Amersham 21121
(STD code 024 03)

Vocational Course, 2 years
1 yr foundation or similar + 5 'O's
Regional diploma

Birkenhead

Wirrall College of Art & Design Adult Studies
Park Road North
Birkenhead
Merseyside L41 4EZ
Tel: Liverpool 647 9236/7
(STD code 051)

Vocational Course/
Industrial Ceramics
3 yrs
3 'O's
College Certificate CIC

Birmingham

City of Birmingham Polytechnic Art & Design Centre
New Corporation Street
Birmingham B4 7DX
Tel: Birmingham 359 6721
(STD code 021)

BA(Hons) 3D design CNAA
ceramics with glass.
1 year foundation,
5 'O's. 18+

Bolton

Bolton Technical College Department of Art and Design Studies
Hilden Street
Bolton BL2 1JB
Tel: Bolton 31411
(STD code 0204)

Vocational course 2-4 years
3 'O's
College Diploma
College Higher Diploma LSD-C

Bournemouth

Bournemouth & Poole College of Art
Royal London House
Lansdowne
Bournemouth BH1 3JL
Tel: Bournemouth 20772
(STD code 0202)

Specialist option
DATEC General Art
and Design Diploma

Braintree

Braintree College of Further Education
Church Lane
Braintree
Essex
Tel: Braintree 21711
(STD code 0376)

Vocational course/studio pottery.
2 or 3 years, 3 'O's
College Diploma and East Anglian Diploma
in Design (studio pottery); 3rd year to
Licentiate of Society of Designer Craftsmen

Brighton

Brighton Polytechnic Faculty of Art and Design
Grand Parade
Brighton BN2 2JY
Tel: Brighton 604141
(STD code 0273)

BA(Hons) CNAA-wood, metal, ceramics and
plastics course. 3 years full time.
Normally 1 year foundation + 5'O's
Direct entry 2 'A's + 3 'O's.

Bristol

Bristol Polytechnic Faculty of Art and Design
Clanage Road
Bower Ashton
Bristol BS3 2JU
Tel: Bristol 660222
(STD code 0272)

BA(Hons) Ceramics

Chesterfield

Chesterfield College of Art & Design
Sheffield Road
Chesterfield S41 7LL
Tel: Chesterfield 70271
(STD code 0246)

DATEC Higher Diploma in Design Crafts
(Studio Ceramics)

Carlisle	**Cumbria College of Art & Design** Brampton Road Carlisle Cumbria CA3 9AY Tel: Carlisle 25333 (STD code 0228)	DATEC Higher Diploma: Ceramics Craft Option
Corsham	**Bath Academy of Art** Corsham Court Corsham, Wiltshire Tel: Corsham 712571 (STD code 0249)	BA(Hons) Ceramics
Derby	**Derby College of Art & Technology** Kedleston Road Derby DE3 1GB Tel: Derby 47181 (STD code 0332)	DATEC Higher Diploma in Design Crafts (Studio Ceramics). 2 years. DATEC Diploma, Foundation, 'A' levels
Eastbourne	**College of Art & Design** Eversley Court St. Anne's Road Eastbourne, Sussex Tel: Eastbourne 28674 (STD code 0323)	Vocational course/Studio Pottery and Ceramic Sculpture. Diploma SIAD Ceramics. LSD-C Studio Pottery
Epsom	**Epsom School of Art & Design** Ashley Road Epsom, Surrey KT18 5BE Tel: Epsom 28811 (STD code 03727)	2 year DATEC Diploma in Designer Crafts. 2 year DATEC Higher Diploma
Exeter	**Exeter College of Art & Design** Earl Richards Road North Exeter EX2 6AS Tel: Exeter 77977 (STD code 0392)	Main Option on BA(Hons) Fine Art course. Vocational Pottery for Mature Students
Farnham	**West Surrey College of Art and Design** The Hart Farnham, Surrey Tel: Farnham 722441 (STD code 02513)	BA(Hons) Ceramics with supporting studies, shorter courses for self-funding advanced students will be considered and research facilities for established crafts people.
Harrogate	**Harrogate College of Arts & Adult Studies** 2 Victoria Avenue Harrogate HG1 1EL Tel: Harrogate 62446 (STD code 0423)	DATEC Diploma in studio ceramics. 2 years full time. Good general education and prior experience in ceramics preferable.
Hereford	**Herefordshire College of Art & Design** Folly Lane Hereford Tel: Hereford 3359 STD code 0432)	Vocational course/ceramics TOPS 1 year intensive course. 3 years 3 'O's (1 academic). College Diploma LSD-C.
High Wycombe	**Buckinghamshire College of Further Education** **School of Art & Design** Queen Alexandra Road High Wycombe HP11 2JZ Tel: High Wycombe 22141 (STD code 0494)	BA(Hons) Ceramics with glass
Lancaster	**Preston Polytechnic School of Art & Design** Lancaster Annexe Meeting House Lane Lancaster LA1 1TH Tel: Lancaster 68121 (STD code 0524)	Ceramic based product Design Vocational/3 yr Sandwich Polytechnic Diploma & LSIA 5 'O's or equivalent + foundation course or 'A' levels

Loughborough	**Loughborough College of Art & Design** Radmoor Loughborough Leicestershire Tel: Loughborough 261515 (STD code 0509)	BA(Hons) ceramics
Lowestoft	**Lowestoft School of Art** **College of Further Education** St. Peters Street Lowestoft Suffolk NR32 2NB Tel: Lowestoft 83521 (STD code 0502)	DATEC Diploma and Higher Diploma (to be confirmed). 2 years + 2 years. Preferably 3 'O's or equivalent. 3 years to EADDes + 1 year to CIC, DSIAD
Manchester	**Manchester Polytechnic Faculty of Art & Design** Cavendish Street All Saints Manchester M15 6BR Tel: Manchester 228 6171 (STD code 061)	BA(Hons) 3D Design Wood/metal/ceramics/glass (C.N.A.A.)
Middlesbrough	**Cleveland College of Art & Design** Green Lane Middlesbrough Cleveland Tel: Middlesbrough 821441 (STD code 0642)	Design Crafts Certificate DATEC GAD/GVD Diploma (diagnostic ceramics)
Nuneaton	**North Warwickshire College of Technology & Art** Hinckley Road Nuneaton Warwickshire CV11 6BH Tel: Nuneaton 349321 (STD code 0682)	DATEC Diploma in Three Dimensional Design (Ceramics)
Preston	**Preston Polytechnic** **Faculty of Art & Design** St. Peter's Square Preston PR1 7BX Tel: Preston 22141 (STD code 0772)	2 year Higher DATEC Diploma Wood/metal/ceramics
Redruth	**Cornwall College of Further & Higher Education** Redruth Cornwall Tel: Camborne 712911 (STD code 0209)	DATEC Diploma General Vocational Design DATEC Diploma Design/Crafts Ceramics. 2 years, 3 'O' levels grade C or above, or grade 1 CSE's. DATEC Higher Diploma Ceramics. 2 years. As above plus DATEC Diploma or Foundation Course.
Rochester	**Medway College of Design** Fort Pitt Rochester, Kent ME1 1DZ Tel: Medway 44815 (STD code 0634)	2 year Diploma Course Design Crafts, Ceramics. Normally 16 years + 3 'O' levels. 2 year Higher Diploma Course Design Crafts Ceramics. Normally 18 years + 5 'O' levels
Stafford	**Stafford College of Further Education** Earl Street Stafford Staffordshire ST16 2QR Tel: Stafford 42361 (STD code 0785)	Vocational Courses/Industrial Ceramics 3 years for C.I.C./S.I.A.D. 5 'O's 2 years for DATEC Diploma in 3D Design Ceramics, 3 'O's 2 years for DATEC Higher Diploma in Ceramic Design Technology. Entry: Diploma in 3D Ceramic Design or comparable qualification.

ke-on-Trent	**North Staffordshire Polytechnic** Department of Design (Ceramics) College Road Stoke on Trent ST4 2DE Tel: Stoke on Trent 45531 (STD code 0782)	BA(Hons) Design, multi-disciplinary design course including specialisation in Industrial Ceramics, Hand Pottery, Ceramic Sculpture, Glass
ourbridge	**Stourbridge College of Technology & Art** Church Street Stourbridge West Midlands DY8 1LY Tel: Stourbridge 78531 (STD code 038 43)	BA(Hons) 3D Design, Glass with ceramics
olverhampton	**The Polytechnic Wolverhampton** **Faculty of Art & Design** North Street Wolverhampton WV1 1DT Tel: Wolverhampton 29911 (STD code 0902)	BA(Hons) ceramics LSD-C

WALES

ardiff	**South Glamorgan Institute of Higher Education** **Faculty of Art & Design** Howard Gardens Cardiff CF2 1SP Tel: Cardiff 482202 (STD code 0222)	MA Ceramics BA(Hons) Ceramics
Carmarthen	**Dyfed College of Art** Job's Well Road Carmarthen Dyfed Tel: Carmarthen 5855 (STD code 0267)	Vocational Course in Ceramics 4 years full time, normally 5 'O's. 1 year exemption for foundation students. Successful students may be additionally assessed externally for Diploma membership of the SIAD and/or for LSD-C
Newport	**Gwent College of Higher Education** **Faculty Art & Design** Clarence Place Newport, Gwent NPT 0UW Tel: Newport 55907 (STD code 0633)	BA(Hons) Fine Art
Wrexham	**NE Wales Inst Higher Education** School of Creative & Expressive Arts 49 Regent Street Wrexham, Clwyd Tel: Wrexham 56601 (STD code 0978)	2 years Diploma/Certificate 3 'O's or 3 CSEs — Folio

SCOTLAND

Aberdeen	**Grays School of Art** Robert Gordons Institute of Technology Garthdee Road Aberdeen AB9 2QD Tel: Aberdeen 572811 (STD code 0224)	Degree course ceramics with sculpture 4 yrs. 3 'H's inc. Eng + 2 'O's or 2 'A's inc. Eng + 3 'O's. Diploma of Art
Dundee	**Duncan of Jordanston College of Art** School of Design Perth Road Dundee DD1 4HT Tel: Dundee 23261 (STD code 0382)	Degree course/pottery & ceramics 3 years. Foundation course + normally 2 'A's + 3 'O's or 3 SCE 'H's + 2 SCE 'O's. BA/BA Hons. Degree

Edinburgh	**Edinburgh College of Art** School of Design & Crafts Lauriston Place Edinburgh EH3 9DF Tel: Edinburgh 229 9311 (STD code 031)	Degree course/ceramics 3 SCE 'H's inc. Eng. 2SCE 'O's (C band or above). 2 GCE 'A's 3 GCE 'O's (inc. Eng. at 'A' or 'O'). BA in Design
Glasgow	**Glasgow School of Art** 167 Renfrew Street Glasgow G3 6RQ Tel: Glasgow 332 9797 (STD code 041)	Degree course/ceramics 2 SCE 'H's inc. Eng. + 2 'O's BA(Hons)/BA Design (Ceramics)

NORTHERN IRELAND

Newtownabbey	**Ulster Polytechnic** Jordanstown Newtownabbey Co. Antrim Tel: Newtownabbey 1245131 (STD code 023)	BA(Hons) ceramics

Post Graduate Courses in Ceramics

London	**Goldsmiths' College** New Cross SE14 6NW	Advanced Diploma in Art & Design ceramics
	Royal College of Art Kensington Gore SW7 2EU Tel: 01-584-5020	M Des RCA/MA RCA Ceramic Product Design. Architectural Ceramics. Craft Ceramics. Decoration. Research into mixed materials and technology.
Stoke-on-Trent	**North Staffordshire Polytechnic** Department of Design (Ceramics) College Road Stoke on Trent Staffordshire ST4 2DE Tel: Stoke on Trent 45531 (STD code 0782)	MA Design (Ceramics) 2 year sandwich course
Cardiff	**South Glamorgan Institute of Higher Education** **Faculty of Art & Design** Howard Gardens Cardiff CF2 1SP Tel: Cardiff 482202 (STD code 0222)	MA Ceramics
Aberdeen	**Grays School of Art** Robert Gordons Institute of Technology Garthdee Road Aberdeen AB9 2QD Tel: Aberdeen 572811 (STD code 0224)	Ceramics with Sculpture 1 yr post graduate diploma Diploma of Art or BA CNAA
Edinburgh	**Edinburgh College of Art** School of Design & Crafts Lauriston Place Edinburgh EH3 9DF Tel: Edinburgh 229 9311 (STD code 031)	Diploma in Ceramics. A one year course normally requiring good honours degree for entrance.
Glasgow	**Glasgow School of Art** 167 Renfrew Street Glasgow G3 6RQ Tel: Glasgow 332 9797 (STD code 041)	1 year Degree or equivalent MA(Design) Diploma of postgraduate studies

Local Pottery Societies

Local pottery societies are a good way of making contact with other potters. The following list is by no means complete but further addresses can probably be obtained from local libraries or adult education institutes.

South Wales Potters
Gail Stewart
Brook Cottage
Llanvetherine
Nr. Abergavenny
Gwent NR6 8RG

Midland Potters Association
Doug Wensley
4 St. Albans Road
Bestwood Village
Nottingham NG6 8TQ

Merseyside Guild of Potters
Ray Hargreaves
Rosehill Pottery
2 Hartsbridge
Southport, Merseyside

Northampton Potters
Caroline Pinner
The Pottery
Overstone Park
Northampton

Wey Ceramics
Jean Maffey
South Weald
Blacknest
Alton
Hampshire

Kent Potters Association
Christina Ransley
Flat 1, Elmsfield Lodge
Rookery Lane
Bromley Common
Kent

Wealden Pottery Group
Tom Wels
Old Lands Leys
Herons Ghyll
Uckfield
Sussex. TN22 4BY

East Anglian Potters
Alan Baxter
The White House Studio
Somersham
Ipswich
Suffolk

Dacorum & Chiltern Potters Guild
Pauline L. Ashley
10 The Heath
Radlett, Herts

Northern Potters Association
Colin Woodcock
8 Moorlands
Prudhoe, Northumberland NE42 5LS

Scottish Potters Association
Pat Charles
240 Colinton Mains Road
Edinburgh EH13 9BU

Southern Ceramic Group
Margaret Brooks
50 Ashdene Road
Ashurst, Hants. SO4 2BW

Guild of North Wales Potters
John Hughes
The Cottage
Llanrheadr
Denbigh, Clwyd

Free information

Nowadays most potters' merchants supply lavishly illustrated catalogues free of charge that, as well as listing their materials and equipment, contain much useful information. Write for them all. (Most suppliers advertise regularly in *Ceramic Review*). For the more advanced student Borax Consolidated Ltd., Borax House, Carlisle Place, London SW1, publish an excellent book *Ceramic Glazes*. This, also, is available free of charge.

Overseas Societies

Readers wishing to contact potters when travelling abroad can write to the societies listed below, who will be able to provide addresses. Some of these societies have issued an illustrated directory of their members' work.

Pottery Societies

Europe

Craft Potters Society of Ireland
70 Merion Road
Dublin 4, Eire.

Chambres Syndicales des Ceramistes
45 Rue des Petites Ecuries
75010, Paris

Asia

Ceramic Artists Association of Israel
P.O. Box 17095
Tel Aviv, Israel

Australia

Potters' Society of Australia
48-50 Burton Street
Darlinghurst N.S.W. 2010
Australia

Perth Potters Club
Box 3
1 Burt Street
Cottesloe
Western Australia

Geelong Ceramic Group
P.O. Box 96
Belmont, Victoria 3216
Australia

Richmond Potters Group
P.O. Box 65
Richmond,
Queensland 4822

Victoria Ceramic Group
P.O. Box 4096
Spencer Street
Melbourne, Victoria 3001
Australia

Newcastle Ceramic Group
Cooks Hill, NSW 2300
Australia

Albury Wadenga Potters Group
c/o Mrs. H. Winkinson
698 Nenda Avenue
Albury, NSW 2640
Australia

New Zealand

Otago Potters Group
6 Neville Street
Dunedin
New Zealand

Tauranga Potters Group
86 17th Avenue
Tauranga
New Zealand

Canterbury Potters Association
P.O. Box 2193
Christchurch
New Zealand

New Zealand Society of Potters
c/o New Zealand Potter
15 Wadestown Road
Wellington 1
New Zealand

Wanganui Potters Society
44 Fitzherbert Avenue
Wanganui
New Zealand

Canada

Ontario Potters Association
c/o Hamilton & Region Arts Council
140 Yorkurle Ave
Toronto
Ontario M5R 1C2
Canada

Burlington Potters Guild
5242 Cindy Lane
Burlington, Ontario
Canada L7R 2G6

Cariboo Potters Guild
Box 4852
Williams Lake, BC
Canada V2G 2L5

Potters Guild of British Columbia
315 West Cordova Street
Vancouver BCV6 DIE5
Canada

Canadian Guild of Potters
100 Avenue Road
Toronto 5, Canada

Ottawa Guild of Potters
450 Bay Street
Ottawa, Ontario
Canada K1R 6A8

Alberta Potters Association
10916 56 Street
Edmonton
Alberta T6A 2J6
Canada

Thunder Bay Potters Guild
82 Rupert Street
Thunder Bay, Ontario
Canada P7B 3W7

U.S.A.

Hawaii Potters Guild
1212 University Avenue
Honolulu
Hawaii 96826

Ceramic League of Miami
8873 SW 129 Street
Miami, Florida 33176

Information for countries not represented above can be obtained from:

World Crafts Council — United Kingdom
c/o Crafts Council
12 Waterloo Place, London SW1 4AU

People
and
Events

THE LEACH POTTERY

BERNARD LEACH
JANET LEACH

St. Ives, Cornwall.
Phone St. Ives 398

27. XII · 60

Dear Rosemary,

I hasten to let you know that I shall stay in London over Friday Jan. 13th & will therefore be able to come to your gathering that evening. I am afraid Janet, my wife, will have had to return to St. Ives.

A happy N. Year to you & your Mother. We go up for preparations tomorrow & this is written in haste.

Yours

Bernard Leach

Letter from Bernard Leach to Rosemary Wren accepting an invitation to the CPA Winter Party held at the Arts Council Gallery, St. James's Square during the Bernard Leach 50 Year Retrospective Exhibition.

Craftsmen Potters Association of Great Britain Ltd.

President	Pamela, Lady Glenconner
Treasurer	David Winkley

Council 1983 — 1984

Chairwoman	Jane Hamlyn
Vice-Chairman	David Frith
	Paul Barron
	Joan Benjamin (co-opted Associate Member)
	Emmanuel Cooper
	Dorothy Feibleman
	Ruth King
	John Leach
	Eileen Lewenstein
	George Rainer
	David Winkley
	Andrew Young

Association

Accounts	Elsbeth De Silva
Secretary	Marilyn Parker

Craftsmen Potters Shop

Manager	Vivien Whitaker
Assistants	Robert John
	Helen Kingsley
	Tricia Mahoney

Ceramic Review

Editors	Eileen Lewenstein
	Emmanuel Cooper
Editorial Assistant, Advertising	Daphne Matthews
Subscriptions and Books	Marilyn Brown

Past and Present Members

Early records of the association are incomplete and in some instances confusing. Following is a list which we hope includes the names of all who have been full members of the Craftsmen Potters Association at one time or another. Corrections would be appreciated.

Originally anyone owning or renting a workshop and selling work to the public under their own name or seal qualified for full membership. Within a year of opening the Lowndes Court shop, selection on the basis of work was introduced for new applicants, and within a further year a similar selection process was devised for members who had joined before April 1961. Since that date new membership has been subject to selection combined with periodic re-assessment of all members' work.

Adrian Abberley
Katherine M. Aitken
Louise M. Aitken
Brigitta Appleby
Dan Arbeid
Hester Armstrong
Peter Arnold
Mick Arnup
Keith Ashley
Chris Aston
Marigold Austen
Aylesford Pottery
Aylmer R.S. Aylott
Gordon Baldwin
Alan Barrett-Danes
Ruth Barrett-Danes
Paul Barron
Val Barry
Richard Batterham
Svend Bayer
Michael Bayley
Peter Beard
Beverley Bell-Hughes
Terry Bell-Hughes
Tony Benham
Agnes Benson
Maggie Berkowitz
John Berry
Joan Biggs
Audrey Blackman
Carol Blades
Robert Blatherwick
Elsie Blumer
Janet Boston
Charles H. Brett
Helen Brink
J. R. Brooke
Clive Brooker
Bill Brown
Paul Brown
Yvette Brown
Michael Buckland
Kirstie Buhler
Ruth Burchard
Deirdre Burnett
Graham Burr
Ian Byers
Alan Caiger-Smith
David Canter
Michael Cardew

Barbara Cass
Michael Casson
Sheila Casson
John Chalke
Vera Cheesman
Harry F. Clark
Kenneth Clark
Jenny Clarke
Derek Clarkson
Margery Clinton
Michael Cole
Walter V. Cole
Russell Collins
Barbara Colls
Ernest Collyer
Joanna Constantinidis
Delan Cookson
Emmanuel Cooper
Maureen Cooper
Waistell Cooper
Aubrey Coote
Daphne Corke
Jean M. Cornwallis
Keith G. Corrigan
Molly Coryn
B. J. Cotes
Suzi Cree
Stella R. Crofts
Peter Crotty
John Dan
Robi Dart
Dartington Pottery Training Workshop
John Davidson
Leslie G. Davie
Clive Davies
G. Birt Davies
John Davies
Derek Davis
Bob Dawe
Clare Dawkins
Sally Dawson
Peter Dick
Mike Dodd
Micky Doherty
Lawrence Dowdall
Ruth Duckworth
Rosemary Dugdale-Bradley
Elizabeth Duncombe
Adam G Dworski
Una Dyer

Geoffrey Eastop
Dave Edmonds
David Eeles
Marion Ehlers
Siddig El'Nigoumi
Derek Emms
Miguel Espinosa
Howard Evan
Ronald Everson
J. Farleigh
George Fathers
Dorothy Feibleman
Murray Fieldhouse
Raymond Finch
John T. Fisher
Tina Forrester
Audrie H. Forse
Audrey Forse
Robert Fournier
Sheila Fournier
Sylvia des Fours
Ruth Franklin
R. Freeman
Alan Frewin
David Frith
Annete Fuchs
Tessa Fuchs
Geoffrey Fuller
T. Fuller
Margaret Galbraith
Tony Gant
Ray Gardiner
Ian Garrett
Wilfred Gibson
Ian Godfrey
Anne Gordon
William Gordon
Alan Spencer Green
Pamela Greenwood
Ian Gregory
Arthur Griffiths
Lavender Groves
Anna Hagen
Shoji Hamada
Frank Hamer
Jane Hamlyn
Henry F. Hammond
Gwyn Hanssen
Louis Hanssen
Keith Harding

remy Harper
Muriel Harris
Frederic Harrop
Ian Heaps
Gwen Henderson
Daphne Henson
Joan Hepworth
David Hilton
Andrew Holden
Rozelle Holden
G. T. Holland
Nicholas Homoky
Gwen Horlick
Thomas W. Howard
Agnete Hoy
John Huggins
Glynn Hugo
Evelyn Ingham
Neil Ions
G. M. Jackson
John Jelfs
Chris Jenkins
Richard Jenkins
David Lloyd Jones
Muriel Tudor Jones
Stephanie Kalan
Nora Kay
Walter Keeler
Lawrence Keen
Colin Kellam
Dorothy Kemp
Jeremy Kemp
Danny Killick
Maureen E. Koppenhagen
Dennis Lacey
Violet E. Lakeman
Dennis Lane
Peter Lane
Bernard Leach
David Leach
Janet Leach
John Leach
Michael Leach
Trentham de Leliva
Eileen Lewenstein
Margery Clare Littleboy
Trevor Logan
John Lomas
Gillian Lowndes
Rosemary McCay
Andrew McGarva
John McLellan
Una McLellan
Christopher Magarshack
Mal Magson
G. G. Makin
Jim Malone
John Maltby
Victor Margrie
Anthony Markes
Margaret Marks
Ray F. S. Marshall
Scott Marshall
West Marshall
Audrey Martyn
Frank Matthews
Leo Matthews
Brendan Maund
Geoffrey G. Maund
Denis R. May

Peter Meanley
William Mehornay
Eric Mellon
Paul Metcalfe
Rosemary Middleton
David Miller
Mary Mitchell-Smith
Esmie Moody
Denis Moore
Gerrard H. Morgan
Anthony Morris
David Morris
Joan Motley
Diana Myer
Frances Nash
Pamela Nash
C. Bryant Newbold
Godfrey Newcomb
Mary Newcomb
Bryan Newman
Mary Nicoll
Eileen Nisbet
Margaret Obee
Magdalene A. N. Odundo
Hoon Ai Ooi
George Owen-Jones
Cicely Parker
Warwick Parker
Judith Partridge
Colin Pearson
Betty Perrett
Peter Phillips
Baajie Pickard
Helen Pincombe
Ian Pirie
Alice T. Pisk
Gordon Plahn
Katharine Pleydell-Bouverie
Thomas Plowman
John Pollex
Elisabeth M. Powell
George Rainer
Winifred Rawsthorne
Vicki Read
John Reeve
Stanislas Reychan
Mary Rich
Christine-Ann Richards
Andrew Richardson
Dave Roberts
Frank Robinson
Jim Robison
Bryan Rochford
Mary Rogers
Bernard Rooke
Muriel Rose
Roger Ross-Turner
Godfrey Rubens
Fay Russell
Jane Sarene
Paula Schneider
David Scott
Maria Seviers
Ray Silverman
Peter Simpson
John Singleman
Michael C. Skipwith
Mildred Slatter
Marga Sleja
Frank Smith

Peter Smith
John Solly
Reg. G. Southcliffe
Gary Standige
Ann Stannard
Peter Starkey
Janet B. Stebbing
Anthony Sterckx
Eric Stockl
Peter Stoodley
Debora Storch
Warren Storch
Harry Horlock Stringer
H. J. C. Sturton
Helen Swain
Geoffrey Swindell
Janice Tchalenko
Byron Temple
Anne Thalmessinger
Pauline M. Thompson
Owen Thorpe
E. G. Timms
Vera Tollow
Marianne de Trey
John Turner
Kate Turner
Angela Verdon
Sally Vinson
James F. Walford
Alan Wallwork
Sarah Walton
John Ward
Thomas Ward
F. J. Watson
David Weake
K. G. F. Webb
Robin Welch
Daphne Wells
Tony Weston
Westwood Pottery
Mary White
Elizabeth Whitehouse
Geoffrey Whiting
Eleanor Whittall
Sheila Willison
David Winkley
Molly Winterburn
Violet L. Witherby
Nigel Wood
Denise K. Wren
Rosemary D. Wren
Muriel Wright
Takeshi Yasuda
Poh Chap Yeap
Andrew Young
Joanna Young
Monica Young
W. M. Young
Douglas Zadek

Honorary Members

David Canter
Michael Cardew
Shoji Hamada
Pan Henry
W. A. Ismay
Ladi Kwali
Bernard Leach
Denise Wren

Recent reports and notices from the Red Rose Guild of Craftsmen and the Crafts Centre of Great Britain show concern over the Purchase Tax impositions. The Red Rose Guild invites the opinions of members. The Crafts Centre held an open potters' meeting under the chairmanship of Mr. Heber Mathews and with a representative of the Rural Industries Bureau (Mr. O. W. Lipton) on the platform. The meeting disclosed that a diversity of personal interests, within and outside the craft, are pursuing the problem independently and with optimism that some relief will ultimately be obtained. The Financial Times made out an excellent case for the general withdrawal of the tax.

Report from 'Pottery Quarterly' 9, Spring 1956.

An Important Meeting of Potters

will be held on the 16th February, 1957, at 2.30 p.m.,

at the Art Workers' Guild, 7 Queens Square, W.C.1.

At the Export Pottery Display held last year at the Rural Industries Bureau a Working Party was appointed to consider the formation of an Association of Craftsmen Potters. The Working Partys Report may be obtained from the Acting Secretary—O. W. Lipton, Rural Industries Bureau, 35 Camp Road, Wimbledon Common, London, S.W.19—and will be considered at this meeting, which is of the utmost importance to all potters.

From 'Pottery Quarterly' 12, Winter 1956.

Kiln Building at Loseley Potters Camp 1975.

THE CRAFTSMEN POTTERS'
OF GREAT BRITAIN

invite the support of every individual potter and small pottery workshop in this stimulating venture recently formed. The need for a national organisation of this kind has for long been evident; so has the fact that a successful one could be of immeasurable benefit to potters of all kinds. At last the opportunity is offered to realise this very desirable object. It is certain that our numbers are much greater than is generally realised. There is no doubt that a potential exists from which a really effective representative body could be built. It is sincerely hoped that, after reading some of the Association's aims, briefly set out below, you will be convinced that this bold enterprise fully merits your practical support.

HEADQUARTERS FACILITIES: In London an association showroom-shop to which members could send their wares for display and sale without jury. A library of pottery books and technical information with provision for study on the spot and available postally to members unable to call. Accommodation for craft meetings, conferences, demonstrations and for members to meet socially.

PUBLIC RELATIONS: By all possible means (press, advertising, radio, &c.) keep craft pottery in the public eye. Advise and help members on their participation in exhibitions. Publish a directory of members and member-potteries. Circulate craft news and information. Establish advantageous relationships with other organisations.

MARKETING: Advise and assist in finding markets, making contacts and contracts, suitability of wares, exporting, customers' credit standing, hire-purchase, taxation.

OFFICIAL: Interpret Ministerial orders, watch prospective legislation and keep Government departments informed on potters' views and make representations on their behalf. Advise and assist potters in any difficulty arising over conformation with laws and by-laws. Sponsor and canvass support for any desirable changes in same.

TRADE RELATIONS: Obtain concessionary terms from manufacturers for members buying equipment and materials and/or a co-operative purchasing scheme through the Association. Arrange for insurance and legal advice.

APPRENTICESHIP: Establish a scheme whereby employees in member potteries could qualify for documentary endorsement of their having attained a recognised standard of competence in the craft.

OVERSEAS LIAISON: Maintain contacts with fellow-workers abroad, exchange news and technical information, arrange for reception of overseas visitors and introductions for members going abroad.

This necessarily abbreviated outline surely indicates that the Association has an ambitious programme. Yet, even at this very early stage, some parts of it are actually being operated! There is no reason whatsoever why there should not soon be a fully functioning organisation.

Apply for details to the Secretary, The Craftsmen Potters' Association of Great Britain, 35 Camp Road, Wimbledon, S.W.19.

From 'Pottery Quarterly' 14, Summer 1957.

Denise Wren explaining the mysteries of the Oxshott Saltglaze Kiln at an early Potters Day.

Craftsmen Potters Association Events

No complete record of the visits, parties and general events organised by the CPA has been kept. This list has been drawn up from existing records.

1956
July 25   Meeting Rural Industries Bureau, Wimbledon Working Party Appointed

1957
February   Inaugural Meeting Art Workers Guild, London

1958
January   Meeting Caxton Hall London
February   Foundation Meeting Royal Hotel London
October   Potters Day at Oxshott. Visit Rye Pottery

1959
October   Potters Day at Oxshott

1961
January   Party Arts Council Gallery St. James's Square London, to celebrate Bernard Leach 50 year Retrospective
July   Visit to Muriel Wright at Aldbeurgh
October   Potters Day Aylesford Priory
December   Party Finnish Exhibition Victoria and Albert Museum, London

1962
May   R. D. Wren sent as delegate to International Academy of Ceramics meeting in Prague
November   Party Ancient Peruvian Art. Arts Council Gallery, St. James's Square, London

1963
September   Full Members Meeting, Potters Croft, Oxshott

1964
February   Meeting at the Horniman Museum.
May   R. D. Wren sent as delegate to I.A.C. meeting in Geneva
September   Visit to Wrecclesham Pottery

1965
May   Annual Party at Commonwealth Institute.

1966
March   Party at Ken Clark's Studio, London W1
July   Potters Day at Taggs Yard, Barnes, London

1967
September   CPA Group Visit to I.A.C. meeting and exhibition in Istanbul
December   Opening of New Shop. 7 Marshall Street, London W1

1968
October   Potters Day at Taggs Yard, Barnes, London

1970
October   C.P.A. Film Survey. 23 Films. Stanhope Institute, London, NW1.

1972
September   Full Members Weekend Meeting, West Dean College, West Sussex.

Colin Kellam demonstrating, Potters Camp 1975.

Jerome Abbo demonstrating, Potters Camp 1973.

John Leach demonstrating in the Marshall Street shop, October 1981.

1973

May   Potters Camp at Loseley Park, Surrey. Weeker event.

1975

May   Potters Camp at Loseley Park, Surrey. Weeken event.

1976

October   Meeting at Dillington House for Full Members. Weekend event.

1977

September   C.P.A. Film Festival. University of York. 50 films. Weekend event.

1978

April   C.P.A. Potters Group visit to China.

July   Weekend Meeting, West Dean College, West Sussex.

1979

February   Third C.P.A. Film Festival at Stanhope Institute, London NW1

1980

April   Weekend Workshop at West Dean. Jane and Ted Hamlyn, John Maltby, Peter Starkey and Sarah Walton. For Associate Members.

September   C.P.A. Full Members Weekend Symposium at Dartington with Harry Davis, David Eeles and Derek Emms.

October   One Day Raku at Sudbury Hall, with Susan and Steven Kemenyffy.

1981

April   C.P.A. Second Group Visit to China

April   Potters' Day at Michelham Priory, Sussex

October   Workshop Weekend at West Dean, West Sussex

October   John Leach Shop Demonstration

December   John Pollex Shop Demonstration

1982

February   Shop Demonstration by Michael Casson

May   Potters Camp at Loseley Park, Surrey. Weekend event

June   Neil Ions Shop Demonstration

July   Mary Rogers demonstrating handbuilding at the C.P.A. shop

1983

September   West Dean Weekend event

October   'Studio Ceramics Today' C.P.A. Silver Jubilee

November   Exhibition at the Victoria and Albert Museum

C.P.A. Lectures and Meetings

This list of meetings and lectures arranged by the Craftsmen Potters Association illustrates the scope and breadth of the subjects covered. No systematic record of all meetings has been made: this list has been compiled from available information.

1960
'Handles, Spouts and Knobs' Michael Casson (October)
'Glazes' Discussion (November)
'Pots and Potters of West Africa' Michael Cardew (December)

1961
'Pottery Bodies' William Gordon and Henry Hammond (February)
'Glaze Formula' Dennis Moore (February)
'Income Tax' H. Maggs (April)
'Throwing' Rosemary Wren, Michael Casson, David Eeles (June)
'Teaching in Schools' Peter Arnold (July)
'Make Your Own Tools' Michael Casson and Lawrence Keen (August)
'Starting Your Own Pottery' Ray Marshall (September)
'Geology and Ceramics' Tour of Exhibition (December)

1962
'Pottery from Ancient Peru' Cottie Burland (February)
'Lids, Knobs and Spouts' Gwyn Hanssen (March)
'The Early Wares of China and Korea' Fujio Koyama (April)
'Coiling' by Ladi Kwali. Introduced by Michael Cardew (June)
Report from Prague Exhibition (July)
'Potters Photography' Robert Fournier and John Anderson (August)
'Potters' Minerals' Mr. Bettley (October)

1963
'Turning' Anita Hoy, Rosemary Wren and Harry Horlock Stringer (January)
'Wood Ashes' Katharine Pleydell-Bouverie, Eleanor Whittal, Denise Wren and Waistel Cooper (February)
'Design, The Anti-Craft Approach' Paul Brown (March)
'Ash Glazes' Symposium Geoffrey Whiting, Denis Moore, Michael Buckland and Frank Hamer (April)
'Pottery Decoration' Michael Casson and Alan Caiger-Smith (May)
'Artists of Arnhem Land' Film and Talk David Attenborough (July)
'Pottery in Uganda' Bruce Kent (July)
'Ceramic Glazes' D. A. Holdridge. Four Lectures (September, October, November, January)

1964
'Isaac Button' Film and Talk. Isaac Button, John Anderson and Robert Fournier (March)

1965
'The Common Ground, if any, Between Studio and Industrial Pottery' Murray Fieldhouse, Kenneth Clark, Lord Queensberry, Richard Parkinson (April)
'Throwing' Murray Fieldhouse, Michael Casson and others (June)
'Japanese and Korean Pots' Bernard Leach (November)

1966
'The Education of the Professional Potter' Murray Fieldhouse, Gilbert Harding-Green, Victor Margrie (January)
'Glazes' Katharine Pleydell-Bouverie, Paul Barron (March)
'American Pottery Today' Daniel Rhodes (June)
'Potting in New Zealand' Harry Davis (June)

1967
'Pottery in West Africa' Michael Cardew (Three talks January, February, March)
'French Potters' Gwyn Hanssen (February)
'Japan Today' Film. Michael and Shelia Casson, Peter Rushforth (May)
'New Guinea Potters' Film and Talk by Margaret Tuckson (September)

1968
Report on the International Exhibition of Contemporary Ceramics at Istanbul (March)
'Raw Materials for Bodies and Glazes' Harry Davis (Two part talk July)

1970
'Decoration' Michael Casson, Shelia Fournier and Alan Caiger-Smith (March)

1971
'Eighteenth Century Staffordshire Potters' John Cushion (April)
'Pug-Mill and Clay Dryer' Harry Davis (Two talks July)
'Clay from Tradition to Protest' Jan de Rooden (October)

1972
'David Leach – Potter' David Leach (April)
'Natural Dyes of Peru' Barbara Mullins (May)
'Geoffrey Whiting' and 'Ladi Kwali' Films plus Talk by Robert Fournier (June)
'A Tin-Glaze Workshop Today' Alan Caiger-Smith (December)

1973
Brains Trust on Technical Subjects. Emmanuel Cooper, Robert Fournier, Derek Royle (February)
Brains Trust on Workshop Practice. Harry Horlock Stringer, David Eeles, Barbara Cass, Peter Dick (March)
'Nigerian Pottery' Sylvia Leith-Ross, Michael Cardew, Michael O'Brien, Peter Dick, Ian Auld (September)
'Kilns and Firing' Forum. Colin Kellam, Graham Harvey, Wally Keeler, David Winkley (November)

THE CRAFTSMEN POTTERS ASSOCIATION OF GREAT BRITAIN
LIMITED

3, LOWNDES COURT, CARNABY STREET, LONDON, W.1   Tel: GERrard 7605

Hon. Secretary: David Canter

EVENING MEETINGS
At 7.45 p.m. For FULL, ASSOCIATE & STUDENT MEMBERS

For your convenience the Shop will remain open
from the normal closing time, until the talk.
* * * * * * * * * * * *

SATURDAY Feb 11th.   "What clay do you use"? (earthenware & stoneware)

William Gordon will start the discussion and will hand on
recipes given to him by Artigas. Henry Hammond will ask questions.

THURSDAY Mar 16th.   Glaze Formulae

Denis Moore will explain how to calculate them and how to make
use of them creatively. He strongly recommends the following 3 books.
All obtainable from Foyles, Charing Cross Road, London, W.C.1.

'Chemistry for Beginners'   by Dr. E.J. Holmyard
Dent's Modern Science Series   @ 5/-

'Rutley's Elements of Mineralogy' by George Allen & Unwin 18/-
'A Handbook of Ceramic Calculations' by A.Heath.
Webberley Ltd., Percy Street Works, Stoke-on-Trent. @ 10/-

Denis Moore suggests you bring a paper and pen to make notes.

SATURDAY Apr 15th. at 7. p.m.   Income Tax and Purchase Tax

Mr. H.H. Maggs, Advisory Accountant to the Rural Industries
Bureau, and Mr. O.W. Lipton, Marketing Officer will answer questions
from potters. This is not a lecture on accountancy, but an unparalleled
opportunity for help on Individual Problems from two experts with an
understanding and experience of our ways of working.

Evening Meeting Announcement 1961.

1974
'Chemistry and Manufacture of Glazes' Derek Royle (Harrison
Mayer) (February)
'Journey Through Japan' George Rainer (April)
'Freedom and Discipline in the Crafts' Bob Rogers (July)
'Other Men's Crafts', 'Arts of Village India', 'Living Art of Japan',
'Handicrafts of Japan', 'St. Laurence North: Jean Richard' Four
Films (November)

1975
'An Evening of Inventions' All Members (January)
'Clay for the Potter' C. W. Noake (Potclays) (February)
'Gladstone Pottery Museum' David Sekers (June)

1976
'Modern American Ceramics' Tony Hepburn (April)
'Look Again at Your Glazes' David Green (June)
'Formation and Properties of Clay Bodies' Derek Royle (Harrison
Mayer) (September)

1977
'Raku' John Dickerson (January)
'Establishment of the Pottery at Izcuchaca, Peru' Harry Davis
(March)
'The Relevance of Tradition' John Colbeck (April)
'Contemporary American Ceramics' Eric Gronberg (June)
'New Pottery in Paraguay' Les Sharp and Rory MacLeod (July)
'The Collectors Point of View' W. A. Ismay (October)

1978
'Nigerian Pottery' Shan Bristow (January)
'The Folk Ceramics of Mexico' Professor Art Morrison (June)
'Naturalness in Ceramics' David Hamilton (October)
'Colour in Glazes and Bodies' Ron Carter (Harrison Mayer)
(November)

1979
'Stoneware Glazes by Eastern Methods' Nigel Wood (January)
'Building Equipment from Scrap Materials' Harry Davis
(November)
'Simple Glazes' Emmanuel Cooper (November)

1980
'Onta Pottery and Japanese Craft Movement' Brian Moeran
(January)
'Craft Potters of West and North-West America' Professor Neil
Moss (February)
'An American Potter' Sally Bowen Prange (June)
'Arts of Ancient Peru' Karin Hessenberg (June)
'Canadian Connections' Anne Mortimer and John Chalke
(August)

1981
'Bizen Pottery' Sachiko Tork (April)
Ceramic Collection at the Craft Study Centre Barley Roscoe
(June)
Colin Pearson — potter. Colin Pearson (September)
'A Visit to Japan' Caroline Whyman (October)
'Raku Firing with Charcoal, Coke and Sawdust' Harriet Brisson
(November)
'Gordon Baldwin — Sculptor' Gordon Baldwin (December)

1982
'How We Got Where We Are' Michael Casson (February)
'Saltglaze' Jane Hamlyn (August)
'Electric Kiln Pottery' Emmanuel Cooper (September)
'The Power Kiln' Andrew Holden (November)
'Japanese Art Pottery Movement' Dr. Brian Moeran (December)

1983
'The Victoria and Albert Museum, Contemporay
Ceramics Collection' Dr. Oliver Watson (February)
'Pottery from New Mexico' Joan Weissman (April)
'The International Conference on Ancient Chinese Pottery and
Porcelain' Nigel Wood (May)
'Studio Ceramics' Peter Lane '(September)

Craftsmen Potters Association Exhibitions

No full list of exhibitions arranged by the CPA of members work has been kept. The following lists have been compiled as fully as possible from existing records. Apologies for anyone omitted. The first list is of exhibitions arranged by the CPA, the second list is of exhibitions held in ʿLowndes Court and Marshall Street Shops ʿ London.

ꜱ7
ᵢild of Many Crafts, Blakeney, Norfolk (July/August)
ᵒlkham Hall Wells-next-the-Sea, Norfolk (August)
ᵢiglin Pottery 66 Baker Street and at Heals, Tottenham Court
ᵣad, London (August)
ᵢrdiff (October November)

)58
ᵒrty Members' Travelling Exhibition
4 Hillsleigh Road, London W8, Briglin Pottery, Baker Street,
ᵒndon W1, Holkham Hall, Norfolk, Barrows Stores Ltd
ᵢirmingham, Dunns of Bromley

962
ꜱelected Pots' Herbert Art Gallery and Museum, Coventry (July)

₁963
Selected Pots' La Bourne Gallery, Montmartre Paris (May)

1965
'Selected Pots' International Academy of Ceramics, Musée l'Ariana, Geneva (Spring)
'Selected Pots' Canadian Guild of Potters Toronto Canada
'Selected Pots' Matsuya Store Tokyo Japan (September)

1966
'Selected Pots' Joshua Taylor Cambridge

1978
'Selected Pots' Wolverhampton Art Gallery
(April)

Exhibitions at the Craftsmen Potters Shop, Lowndes Court, London W1.

1960
Ray Finch 'Stoneware' (May, June)
Rosemary D. Wren 'Animals and Birds in Saltglaze' special solus (July)
Murray Fieldhouse 'Stoneware' (August)

1961
Eileen Lewenstein 'Stoneware' (February)
Denis Moore and Michael Buckland (March)
Audrey Blackman 'Stoneware and Earthenware Figures' (March)
Associates Exhibition (July)
John Dan 'Stoneware'
Harry Horlock Stringer 'Earthenware'
Helen Walters 'Saltglaze, Stoneware and Porcelain'
Vera Tollow 'Stoneware' (November)

1962
Teapot Exhibition (April)
Stanislas Reychan 'Pottery Sculpture' (April)
Holkham Studio Pottery (June)
Tony Benham 'Pots' (June)
Michael Skipwith 'Pots' (July)
Peter Lane 'Pots' (August)
Green Dene 'Pottery Pots' (August)
Tessa and Annette Fuchs 'Pots' (September)
Pauline Thompson 'Pots' (September)
Brian Rochford 'Pots' (September)
Alan Wallwork 'Pots' (September October)
Lavender Groves 'Pots' (October)
French Pots and Textiles (November)
David Eeles 'Pots' (November)
Christmas Display (November December)

1963
Eric Stockl 'Pots' (February)
Maria Seviers 'Pots' (February)
Jeremy Harper 'Pots' (March)
Paul and Yvette Brown 'Pots' (March)
Louis Hanssen 'Pots' (May)
All members 'Casseroles' (June)
John Solly 'Pots' (June)
Tom Plowman 'Pots' (September)
Barbara Cass 'Pots' (September)
Tessa and Annette Fuchs (September)
Colin Pearson 'Pots' (September October)
Laurence Keen 'Pots' (October)
Trevor Logan 'Pots' (October)
Denis Moore and Michael Buckland 'Stoneware' (October)
Tony Benham 'Pots' (October)
Bryan Newman and Raymond Silverman (November)

1964
John Berry 'Pots' (March April)
All members 'Pots for Plants' (May June)
Rosemary D. Wren 'Saltglaze and Stoneware' special solus (June)
Group Exhibition. Tony Benham, Keith Harding, Derek Davis, Bryan Rochford, Tessa Fuchs, Anne Thalmessinger, Annette Fuchs. (October)
Michael and Sheila Casson 'Stoneware' special solus (November)

1965
Group Exhibition. Katharine Pleydell-Bouverie, Audrey Blackman, Paul Barron, Michael Buckland, Henry Hammond, Denis Moore. (April May)
Joanna Constantinidis and Pamela Greenwood 'Pots' (May)
All members 'Coffee Pots' (June)
Canadian Guild of Potters 'Canadian Ceramics' (July)
Fay Russell and Emmanuel Cooper 'Stoneware' (September)
Trentham de Leliva 'Stoneware' (October)
Barbara Cass 'Stoneware' Special solus (October November)
George Rainer 'Stoneware' (November)

1966
John Berry 'Ceramic Sculpture'
Keith Harding 'Ceramics' (January)
All members 'Storage Jars' (June)
Geoffrey Whiting 'Stoneware and Porcelain' (September October)
Eric Stockl 'Pots' (October)
David Leach 'Stoneware and Porcelain' (November)

1967
Craftsmen Potters Association of South Wales (May)
Cooking Pot Exhibition open to all members (July)

Exhibitions at Craftsmen Potters Shop, 7 Marshall Street, London W1

1968
Five Potters: Katharine Pleydell-Bouverie, Joanna Constantinidis, Ray Finch, Rosemary D. Wren, Robin Welch (July)
Harry Davis 'Pots' (July)
George Rainer 'Pots' (October)
Six Potters: Alan Wallwork, David Leach, Ian Auld, Colin Pearson, Bryan Newman, Michael Casson (November)

1969
Open Sculpture Exhibition

1970
Bernard Rooke 'Ceramics' (October November)

1971
Coxwold Pottery 'Stoneware and Wood Fired Earthenware' (September)
Harry and May Davis 'Stoneware and Porcelain' (October)
Bryan Newman 'Pots and Sculpture' (November)

1972
South Wales Potters (April)
Alan Caiger-Smith 'Earthenware' (May)
Danny Killick 'Stoneware' (June)
Wally Keeler, Mike Dodd, West Marshall. 'Pots' (September)

1973
Full Members 'Porcelain' (April)
Tessa Fuchs 'Objects' (June)
Danny Killick 'Stoneware' (July August)
Alan Caiger-Smith and Colleagues from Aldermaston (October)
Bryan Newman 'Pots and Sculpture' (November)
Michael Casson

1974
Full Members 'Ceramic Boxes' (March)
Mary Rogers, Mary Rich, John Maltby 'Ceramics' (June)
David Lloyd Jones and Scott Marshall 'Pots' (September)

1975
Full members 'Candlesticks and Candleholders' (February)
Michael Cardew and Associates 'Recent Pots' (April)
Russell Collins and Terry Bell-Hughes 'Recent Work' (October November)

1976
New Members: Val Barry, Dave Edmonds, Dorothy Feibleman, Ian Gregory, Peter Phillips, Andrew Richardson, Geoffrey Swindell. (February)
Six Potters: Paul Barron, Audrey Blackman, Katharine Pleydell-Bouverie, Michael Buckland, Henry Hammond, Denis Moore. (April May)
Full Members 'A Souvenir of Britain' (May)
Deirdre Burnett, Sheila Casson, Janice Tchalenko 'Recent Work' (July)
Joanna Constantinidis 'Recent Work' (September)
Emmanuel Cooper, Derek Davis, Eileen Lewenstein 'Recent Work' (November)

1977
New Members: Peter Beard, Margery Clinton, Tina Forester, John Lomas, Christine Anne Richards (February)
Clive Davies, Andrew Holden, Siddig El'Nigoumi (May)
Peter Dick 'Recent Work' (September)

1978
New Members: Michael Bayley, Margaret Berkowitz, Ray Gardiner, Jane Hamlyn, Gary Standige, Sarah Walton, Andrew and Joanna Young (February)
Modern German Ceramics (March)
Delan Cookson, Geoffrey Eastop, Geoffrey Swindell 'Recent Work' (June)
Full Members 'Tea-pots' (September)
John Davies, Peter Starkey, Derek Emms, David Winkley, 'New Work' (November)

1979
New Members: Mick Arnup, Ruth and Alan Barrett-Danes, Bill Brown, Dartington Pottery Training Workshop, John Jelfs, William Mehornay, John Pollex, Peter Simpson (February)
Eric Mellon, Marianne de Trey, Ray Silverman, Mary White 'Recent Work' (March)
Geoffrey Whiting 'New work' (July)
Ray Finch 'Recent Work' (September)
Full Members 'Bowls' (November)

1980
New Members: Mick Arnup, Ruth Franklin, Ewen Henderson, Alan Heaps, Mal Magson, David Morris, Peter Smith, Nigel Wood (February)
Nick Homoky, Gordon Baldwin, Ruth and Alan Barrett-Danes, Peter Simpson 'New Work' (March)
Full Members 'Jugs' (May)
David Lloyd Jones 'Recent Work' (June)
David Leach 'Stoneware and Porcelain' (September)
Full Members 'Porcelain' (October)
Jane Hamlyn, Jim Malone, Gary Standige 'New Work' (November)

1981
New Members: Chris Ashton, Suzi Cree, Micky Doherty, David Frith, Neil Ions, Ruth King, Andrew McGarva, Dave Roberts, Jim Robison, Warren and Deborah Storch, Byron Temple, John Ward (February)
Val Barry, Peter Beard, Dorothy Feibleman, Peter Meanley 'Recent Work' (March)
Full Members 'Pots for Plants and Flowers' (May)
Terry Bell-Hughes, Dartington Pottery and Alan Pirie 'Recent Work' (July)
Robin Welch 'Recent Work' (June)
Colin Pearson 'New Work' (September)
Peter Smith, Sarah Walton, Andrew and Joanna Young 'Recent Work' (October)

1982
Full Members 'Potters Pots' (February)
David Frith and John Maltby 'New Work' (March)
Ruth Franklyn, Neil Ions, David Robert, John Ward 'Recent Work'
Mary Rogers 'Stoneware and Porcelain' (July)
Wally Keeler 'Saltglaze' (September)
'New French Ceramics' (October)
John Leach and Svend Bayer 'New Work' (November)

1983
New Members' Show: Ian Byers, Miguel Espinosa, John Huggins, David Miller, Angela Verdon, Takesha Yasuda (March)
Janet Leach 'New Work' (April)
Fifteen Full Members 'Decorated Porcelain' (June)
50 Potters 'Studio Ceramics' (September)

THE CRAFTSMEN POTTERS ASSOCIATION
of Great Britain

Invites you to attend the opening, at
11.30 a.m. by the Countess of Leicester
of the

CRAFTSMEN POTTERS SHOP

at 3, Lowndes Court, Carnaby Street, London, W.1

their permanent London exhibition premises
and to the private view of the
inaugural exhibition of
stoneware by

RAY FINCH

of the Winchcombe Pottery

from 12 noon to 5.30 p.m. on Saturday, May 28th 1960

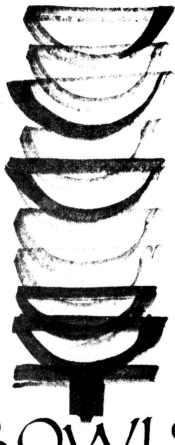

BOWLS
BY MEMBERS OF THE
CRAFTSMEN POTTERS
ASSOCIATION
NOVEMBER·13/24·1979
WILLIAM BLAKE HOUSE
MARSHALL ST·W1
MON/FRI·10·30/5·30 SAT 10·30/5

Janet Leach
New stoneware pots
19–30 April 1983

The Craftsmen Potters Shop
William Blake House
Marshall Street · London W1V 1FD
Telephone 01 437 7605

21 Sept–2 Oct 1982
Salt glazed pots by Walter Keeler

An exhibition of new work
at the Craftsmen Potters Shop
William Blake House
Marshall Street · London W1V 1FD
Telephone 01 437 7605

Craftsmen Potters Association Invitation Cards.